The Ends of Art and Design

Stuart Kendall

Library of Congress Control Number: 2011926653

ISBN 978-0-615-46153-3

Printed in the United States of America.

Design by Martha Blegen

For queries or information, please contact the publisher
at info@infrathin.com

Infra-Thin Press
350 Ann Street
Chadron, Nebraska 69337

Contents

New Struggles. – After Buddha was dead, his shadow was still shown for centuries in a cave – a tremendous, gruesome shadow. God is dead, but given the way of men, there may still be caves for thousands of years in which his shadow will be shown. – And we – we still have to vanquish his shadow, too.

FRIEDRICH NIETZSCHE
The Gay Science §108

The revolution was in the minds of the people, and this was effected from 1760 to 1775, in the course of fifteen years, before a drop of blood was shed at Lexington.

JOHN ADAMS LETTER TO THOMAS JEFFERSON
24 August 1815

Call things by their names.

CONFUCIUS

Preface

Why do we – citizens, consumers, critics, curators, educators – spend so much time and energy, capital and social capital, talking about Fine Art and its various aesthetic analogues, from literature to music, film and beyond, when design, in all of its myriad forms, is manifestly both the most significant force shaping our lives today and so widely misunderstood? This question can be inverted: If the design disciplines give shape to so much of our lives, why don't we spend more time studying, talking, and thinking about them? Why, in short, isn't design at the center of our discourses of cultural self-understanding, in particular as these discourses unfold in our educational institutions and in our museums?

Clearly this is a question of ideology, a question about the ideology that sustains the Fine Art tradition and its institutions and about the way that ideology guides or circumscribes our approach to the design fields, even our failure to approach them. This is an important question, perhaps even a key question for our time, because that ideology is failing the institutions – the schools and museums in particular – that support it and because the design disciplines are themselves undergoing profound internal and external transformations. Changes, in other words, are taking place, whether our prejudices and habits of thought permit us to be aware of them or not.

I'm not suggesting that design has replaced Fine Art in social consciousness. It hasn't and it won't. Design is distinct from Fine Art. It functions in a different way and we live with, through and in relation to the products of the design disciplines in different ways than we lived, and in some ways continue to live with

Fine Art. Most significantly, design is not fundamentally related to representation, either in politics or the arts. Design culture is a different kind of culture, distinct from the modern culture of representation. Understanding the meaning and the implications of this notion will be the principle task of what follows.

If these pages that follow are successful, new approaches to design culture will emerge among designers, design writers, cultural critics across the Humanities, and other citizens and consumers interested in the way we live today. Designers and design writers will be reluctant to use the strategies and tactics of art historical inquiry, including cultural studies methodologies, in considering design and design culture, particularly when those strategies, tactics, and methods treat design as a form of representation. Designers and design writers will also be reluctant to discuss the products of the design fields as purely functional objects or to justify their existence in terms established by technophilia or the idealist culture of functionalist rationalism.

Cultural critics, too, should have something to gain from the pages that follow. Despite the prominence of design in contemporary culture, cultural criticism, including the study of visual culture and the emergent fascination with video games, too often overlooks design or focuses on corners of design production that can be easily appropriated by cultural criticism with familiar tools. By isolating certain types of design for study within specific Humanities fields, cultural critics in Art History, History, American Studies, Philosophy, or literature departments, among other fields, often overlook or misunderstand design culture as a whole or the role of the specific object within that culture. Cultural critics, in short, need to develop more subtle and appropriate methods of understanding design and design culture. Designers and design writers in turn should benefit from these methods and this new understanding of culture.

As should be clear, the purposes of this polemic include ideological, discursive, and institutional critique. If we change the way we think about design we must necessarily change the way that we talk about it, the way we teach it and teach ourselves about it, as well as the ways we celebrate, collect and curate it.

Many cultural critics are, unfortunately, still trained to be allergic to, if not disdainful of design and many designers are trained to be allergic to cultural criticism. Yet design is something that should and in fact does concern all of us, whether as citizens, consumers or creators, and an accurate and nuanced understanding of culture is essential to the practice of design. In an attempt to reach both of these audiences, and other readers besides, I'm writing this pamphlet for a general reader rather than for a specialist in any constrained corner of cultural production or education. Given the power that design has over the way that we live today – and this is not a bad thing – design is something that should interest all of us. I have tried to avoid the jargon of any one field and to avoid the kinds of obscure examples that might interest only specialists. Hopefully the broad outline of the story I have to tell will be familiar to more or less everyone who is kind enough to glance at these pages. I have also eschewed footnotes as much as possible, again in an effort to avoid needless pedantry and obscurity. This pamphlet is intended to be the beginning of a conversation rather than the end of it.

All of this in mind, the terrain traversed herein will, hopefully, be largely familiar; only the perspective will be new. I recognize that it is often easier to see new things in a new way than to see familiar ones afresh. Yet I am prepared to persist. Blithely importing habits of thought from one tradition to another is no more helpful than attempting to invent an entire toolbox of critical inquiry in a vacuum. Put differently, I am not trying to turn design into art or art into design, any more than I am trying to pretend that the radical tradition of social critique has nothing to say to a culture created by design.

Acknowlegments

Through the generous invitations of Kette Thomas at Michigan Technological University and Anthony Raynsford at San Jose State University, portions of this text, in alternate or draft versions, were presented as lectures at those institutions in March and September 2010 respectively. I am grateful to them both, as well as to the audiences for these talks, for their interest, enthusiasm, and productive skepticism.

Deane Tucker and Infra-Thin rescued this project at a key phase of its development. Books cannot live without publishers and this project in particular would not have survived its own extended period of gestation without Infra-Thin, where Martha Blegen brought the book into its fine material form. Small independent publishers like Infra-Thin happily portend the future of thought in American letters.

Finally, it must be said that no thought exists in isolation. Only in the marketplace must we pretend to think for ourselves. Like so much in my life, this project had its origins in a summer of conversations on a mountain outside Santa Fe, New Mexico. That summer and in the seasons since then Vanessa Corrêa and I have discussed, in one way or another, every idea in this book so thoroughly that I can no longer clearly distinguish her intellectual contributions to it from my own. In our case, sharing a life means sharing a vocabulary, a thought, and an orientation to living. Vanessa has also been my first reader, for this as for every other project, and her comments have improved the work immeasurably, without entirely voiding it of the short-comings which are my surely own. I would dedicate this book to her were it not already hers.

The Question of Art and Design

Just over one hundred years ago, in his *Manifesto of Futurism*, F.T. Marinetti proclaimed the presence of a new beauty in the world – the beauty of speed. "A racing car whose hood is adorned with great pipes, like serpents of explosive breath – a roaring car that seems to ride on grapeshot is more beautiful than the *Victory of Samothrace*," he wrote. And museums, he said, are cemeteries.

If we were to take Marinetti seriously, we would have to redirect our gaze, as cultural critics and consumers, away from the paintings in our museums and the books in our libraries, onto the objects that shape and animate our everyday life – objects created by design – and on the experiences those objects promote and provide. It is one thing to seek eternal verities when the world changes very little, generation to generation, and quite another to seek such things – to support or encourage, to promote or even permit – faith in them when the material facts of our experience change as much and as frequently as they do today and have since at least the middle of the nineteenth century.

Marinetti himself did not entirely dispense with art – with an interest in poetry, painting, music, or cinema – but he and the other Italian Futurists attempted to shift its ground and purpose, to transform art into a paean on behalf of a technological culture, a paean to a world created by design. One hundred years later, far more of us own cars than own original works of art. Far more of us drive than read poetry. Yet our self-conscious discourse about ourselves – and even about Marinetti – still remains largely dedicated to the promotion of Fine Art.

A couple of years after Marinetti published his *Manifesto*, Guillaume Apollinaire said something similar in his poem *Zone*. As part of the long poem, he wrote:

*You read the handbills the catalogues the posters singing
aloud
There is poetry this morning and the prose is in the
newspapers*

For Apollinaire, the poetry of the day could be found in the streets, on posters and advertisements. For us, advertizing slogans and commercials are not only some of the most ubiquitous and memorable elements of our daily visual experience, they are some of the most carefully crafted – expensive and profitable – forms of contemporary verbal and visual expression.

One hundred years ago, the hegemony of art over design had already ended. Modern technological civilization had entered a new age. Or it almost had. One hundred years later, our schools and museums remain dedicated to the promotion of Fine Art and uneven in their appreciation, promotion, and criticism of the nature and power of design in contemporary culture. Why is this the case?

For most people, art is art; design is design; and that is all there is to it. And yet, in our culture, these terms persistently rub up against one another at key historical moments, raising themselves as questions as they have again recently. Art and design are at once too proximate to one another and too distant, too similar and too distinct. The relationship between art and design is not idyll, neither insignificant nor fixed. The ideology that gives form to this relationship, that defines and separates these two terms, is persistent but unstable.

At the most basic level, the question of art and design is a question of objects and of actions, of the creative act and the created artifact: to address it is to address the problem of making as a problem for the individual creator and as a problem for the community, whether that community is viewed as a community of autonomous individual subjects, citizens, or consumers. What is it to make something? Why create? For whom? Toward what end?

At another level, the question of art and design is a question of institutions and systems, of charities, governments, corporations, and the public trust. It is a question of the structure and purpose of our institutions of cultural self-consciousness, our museums and institutions of higher education in particular. To question the relationship between art and design is to question the way that we encounter and interact with the objects of our world, but it is also to question the way that we teach ourselves to approach those objects and to live with them, it is to question the nature and type of objects that we venerate, study, and preserve – if we choose to venerate, study, and preserve any objects at all. For me, as an educator, the question of art and design is fundamentally a question of education and of general education in particular, and it is a key question. What do we need to know – and what do we need to teach our children in order for them to know – how to live in the world that we have created for ourselves today?

But to speak of the world that we have created is to speak of the world of design. Learning to live in our created world means learning to negotiate a world of objects and systems created by design and this notion in turn suggests that design education should occupy a far greater place, or play a far greater role, in general education than it does today.

Once again, I am not suggesting that we begin to treat design as if it were art – to simply replace art history with design history, for example. Design objects are fundamentally different from art objects; they cannot be turned into self-sufficient or static representations; they aspire to no autonomous meaning beyond their community of users. An education in design – for consumers, citizens, and designers alike – will be different from an education in the finer points of fine art. Design education proposes an entirely different perspective on the created world and this is part of our topic herein.

The question of art and design is a difficult question to ask, much more difficult than it probably should be. It is difficult in part because it has been asked before, because answers have been offered again and again over the last one hundred and fifty years. These answers – and the perspectives on the question that they imply – now seem at once familiar and fruitless. Hasn't someone already answered this question?

The question is also frequently denied or avoided. It is easy to understand why artists, art critics, art historians, art educators, museum directors, curators, and the governmental and communal supporters of art and the art market would deny or at least downplay the precise nature and pervasive significance of design in contemporary culture and why they would persist in their praise of Fine Art. It is also clear why they would attempt to recuperate design *as* one of the fine arts, through rhetoric and methods of presentation and interpretation.

The products of the Fine Art tradition in the West and many of the aesthetic objects from around the globe that have recently been recuperated by that tradition are of course fascinating and revelatory objects deserving of celebration, preservation, and study, though not always for the reasons they are currently being celebrated or studied. Put differently, the celebrants of these objects obviously have a measure of self-interest at stake in promoting their study, but this self-interest is not unjustified by many of the works themselves. We should not, in other words, expect artists or art historians to be among the most interested advocates of design, nor should we simply discount their interests. The Fine Art tradition is a fascinating tradition.

Designers love it too. Here I'm thinking of the comments one often encounters in some kinds of design writing, when design writers – often designers themselves – loudly advertize their interest in Fine Art, particularly Fine Art derived from design. Design is nice, they suggest, but Art…

This ambivalent relationship is of course at the core of the dialectic of art and design. Fine Art is our cultural idol. Designers idolize it too. Even to the point of denigrating design. Design might be clever or even artistic, but it is not art. The gesture here is one of self-promotion by association. A gesture made by someone with the good taste not to praise himself too mightily.

There are also those designers who aspire to become artists or who actually do so. Design is not art, for them, for they have become artists. A few years ago, I spoke on a conference panel with Sheila Levrant de Brettville, who told our audience that to work for a client is to be oppressed. The statement did not ring true for several of the designers in the audience, who professed to enjoy solving problems for clients, not only for the remuneration but also for the sense of community and shared concern that is entailed in the experience. To suggest that working for clients is oppressive is to focus design practice on materials and methods to the exclusion of key elements of design process and purpose. It is to mistake design for Fine Art.

There are of course other motives for the ambivalent relationship between art and design. Art is good for the design business. Designers can point to Fine Art to prove that they are not frivolous. Art is frivolous, artists are frivolous, or so this story goes; but design is functional, created at the behest of client concerns. Design might be artistic but it isn't art. Designers, in other words, want to place a premium on design, but not too much of a premium. If it's too expensive, clients won't buy it anymore. So long as Fine Art exists, design can be pragmatic, no matter how fun, frivolous, or purely, joyfully, sensuously aesthetic it might actually be.

But these are not the only reasons the question of art and design is denied. Some design writers evidence no interest at all in the question of art or design. For them, contemporary art just isn't very interesting. Design is interesting. Design does things; it solves problems. It gives material shape to the way that we live. Fine Art might offer an amusing entertainment, a pleasant diversion, but design is real. It changes lives. And who can speak of entertainment when so many things in our world manifestly need to be changed, and changed by design?

This is of course iconoclasm. Art is dead: long live design, or rather, long live artless design. This position is rooted in an ideology of functionalist utilitarianism that goes back to the Greeks. In his *Republic*, Plato argued that a representation of something was far less significant than either the actuality of that thing or the idea from which it derived. Plato's critique provided the foundation for three perspectives on things – aestheticism, functionalism, and idealism – and set them in a hierarchy of concern that largely persists to this day.

These three terms – aestheticism, functionalism, and idealism – form a continuum distinguished largely by relative differences. While it is easy to distinguish an aesthetic approach to things (a focus on the sensual aspects of form) from an idealist approach (a focus on the thought which guides or organizes and object or event), it is more difficult to distinguish a functionalist approach from an idealist one, since both are rooted in abstract ideas about objects. It is similarly difficult to distinguish functionalism from aesthetic formalism since both are concerned with form. The middle term – functionalism – is the slippery one and it is of course the key term in discussions of design. Designers and design writers have long been quick to insist that the meaning of a design object is to be found in its fulfillment of a function, even though the appeal of an object of design has never really been so simple.

As an approach to design and as a means of distinguishing design objects from art objects, functionalism is decidedly misleading and limited. Design and design objects have never been purely functional nor have art objects been purely functionless. Acting as if they were won't help us unravel the relationship between art and design nor approach the created objects of our world in a more productive way. Designers and design writers who celebrate design as the embodiment of a pure functionality – or even the outcome of a pure chain of rational decision-making – need to take another look at design.

At this point we might note that the functionalist paradigm in design is dialectically bound to its mirror image: the functionless paradigm that frames Fine Art. If design is functional, Fine Art is, according to the German Idealist philosopher Immanuel Kant, functionless. I particularly appreciate the fluidity with which these positions can be adopted and swapped without changing the fundamental structure of the thought.

According to Kant, Fine Art inspires disinterested contemplation, while design motivates interest. For some of us, this is a statement in praise of Fine Art. For others, it can be understood as favoring design. Each class of objects can either be praised or denied on the basis of this ideological framework even though the framework is and always has been false, or at best only partially true in limited circumstances. Every element of the framework, however positive, is an ideological formation.

According to this ideology, art creates autonomous, thinking, i.e. critical, individuals or subjects while design creates consumers; therefore Fine Art is superior to design. But simultaneously, the world of design is a world of functional, pragmatic realism – the Aristotle to Fine Art's Plato. Thus the consumers of design are to be praised as active agents, alive in a real world. Viewed in its best light, design provides things that people need and produces and distributes them in the most efficacious way possible, for the benefit of both individuals and society as a whole.

The dialectic of art and design here is a dialectic in which each pole can be praised or rejected from the opposite end: promoters of design denigrate art as frivolous, promoters of Fine Art denigrate design as crass and commercial. Yet the whole system, the entire framework is so clearly tautological and solipsistic, so clearly cut off from the real nature of objects in our world that it is hardly ever discussed. Why bother? Art objects have never been purely free; design objects have never been purely functional. How can we break out of this thought pattern?

Technics

Though design is often associated with a functionalist ideal – form follows function, etc. – pure functionalism is more rightly found in the sphere of the applied sciences and engineering, the realm Lewis Mumford called *technics*. The dialectic of art and design, in other words, actually has three key terms – art, design, and technics – with design occupying an amorphous terrain between the other two terms, praised or denigrated for each affiliation in turn.

The Greeks used the word *techne* for the activities and skills of craftsman as well as for the arts of the mind and the fine arts. *Techne* for the Greeks refers to any act of *poiesis*, of making or creation and thus encompasses all three spheres of activity – aesthetic, technical, or abstract – without favoring any one form over another. This is important to remember because it suggests that the Greeks approached the created world from a perspective that is utterly distinct from our own. To see through their eyes would require us to venerate all acts of creation equally, without transforming any created thing into either a functionless idol or a purely functional machine. Such a vision would require a greater degree of fascination or even simple curiosity than many of us, I suspect, possess. It would also entail a sweeping reorganization of our institutions and educational practices and orientation.

The Czech-Brazilian philosopher of design Vilém Flusser discussed the relationship between art, design, and technics in a short essay, "On the Word Design," included in his collection *The Shape of Things: A Philosophy of Design*. After briefly elaborating the histories of the relevant terms, he writes:

> The words *design*, *machine*, *technology*, *ars* and *art* are closely related to one another, one term being unthinkable without the others, and they all derive from the same existential view of the world. However, this internal connection has been denied for centuries (at least since the Renaissance). Modern bourgeois culture made a sharp division between the world of the arts and that of technology and machines; hence culture was split into two mutually exclusive branches: one scientific, quantifiable and 'hard', the other aesthetic, evaluative and 'soft'. This unfortunate split started to become irreversible toward the end of the nineteenth century. In the gap, the word *design* formed a bridge between the two. It could do this since it was an expression of the internal connection between art and technology. Hence in contemporary life, *design* more or less indicates the site where art and technology (along with their respective evaluative and scientific ways of thinking) come

together as equals, making a new form of culture
possible. (19)

Flusser's conclusion – that a new form of culture is possible
through design – is perhaps the most interesting part of the
paragraph, but we will have to come back to it.

Why did modern bourgeois culture separate the world of art
from the world of machines? Modern science and the Fine Art
tradition emerged more or less simultaneously in early modern
Europe. And there are instructive similarities between them.
Both are fascinated with the world of things, yet both seek to
transcend that world – this world – in specific ways. Both extract
meaning from the chaos of phenomena and both leave a trail of
works behind them.

Both are of course products of the Protestant reformation
and the rise of capitalism. Far more thoroughly than Nietzsche's
1882 proclamation of the death of god, Martin Luther's revolution banished the sacred from this world and liberated human will within it. A world without god is a world waiting to be
shaped by human hands, but it is also a fallen world in which
things too are fallen. In such a world, functionlessness is close
to godliness, but so is mastery. The aspiration of the bourgeois
is to transcend the world through a utilitarianism so pure that it
approaches functionlessness. But it is vanity to aspire immediately to functionlessness – such is the fate only of sovereigns and
saints, or is itself a gift of god, a function of the muse. This is the
core ambivalence motivating the dialectic of art and design.

In one of the founding documents of the modern era, *Discourse on Method* (1637), René Descartes advanced an agenda
and method for modern science while also distancing himself
from the aesthetic realm. Fables or stories awaken the mind,
and poetry has a "ravishing delicacy and sweetness," he says,

but such things make one, as it were, a stranger to one's own thoughts. "Fables," he says, "make us imagine many events as possible when they are not." Descartes "delighted in mathematics, because of the certainty and evidence of its reasonings." He devoted himself to research in theoretical and applied science. In announcing his method and its first fruits, Descartes claimed that his research:

> opened [his] eyes to the possibility of gaining knowledge which would be very useful in life, and of discovering a practical philosophy which might replace the speculative philosophy taught in the schools…. Through this philosophy, we could know the power and action of fire, water, air, the stars, the heavens, and all the other bodies in our environment, as distinctly as we know the various crafts of our artisans; and we could use this knowledge – as the artisans use theirs – for all the purposes for which it is appropriate, and thus make ourselves, as it were, the lords and masters of nature.

It is interesting that Descartes borrows the purpose of his science from the work of skilled artisans, though the scope of his project transcends and ultimately comes to subsume theirs. The Cartesian vision of technics is a vision that is built upon a foundation of design and that remains proximate to it. But it is also a vision that renounces any interest in the non-quantifiable realm.

In the Classical age, early modern science and industry could still be subjects of Enlightened fascination among the aristocratic classes, and the acquisition of Fine Art could signal both the power of monarchs and the rising fortunes of the bourgeoisie. But as science and industry truly began to take hold in the middle of the nineteenth century, and as art began to assert its value for its own sake, the tension between the poles of the dialectic became too great. Technics threatened to overwhelm the values of art, to reduce the world to a disenchanted realm of pure resource, what Heidegger would later call a "standing reserve". The Arts and Crafts movement, in its various guises, was born of this tension, with a will to restore the value of work and not just for the bourgeoisie. As William Morris put it, "The cause of Art is the cause of the people... One day, we shall win back Art, that is to say the pleasure of life; win back Art again to our daily labour" (from his book *How We Live and How We Might Live*).

It is obviously enormously significant for our discussion that Morris uses the word Art in reference to all created goods, indeed as a reference to the process of creation, rather than in reference to what we call Fine Art. Morris, in other words, is talking about both art and design. He is attacking the soullessness of most industrially produced or machine made goods, though he does admit the place and utility of the machine in modern life. He is also, and just as intently, suggesting that Art must be a thing of the world rather than solely something for the salon.

His message fascinates me in part for its untimeliness. He wrote at a time when the design fields had yet to truly emerge in even their modern, let alone contemporary forms: a half-century before the foundation of the Bauhaus. And Morris is all but incomprehensible to us now. What he meant by art has almost nothing to do with contemporary art and what he understood by the machine has almost nothing to do with our machines; yet his enemies are still our enemies. Most importantly, though, Morris was unsuccessful in his task. The aesthetic sense he sought to restore to everyday life and labor devolved into mere aestheticism. The rent in culture that he sought to repair has remained open, at least in some ways, though our current cultural configuration, the space of questioning that has opened up for us now, signals that Morris might be ready for reappraisal in the context of both do-it-yourself culture and rapid prototyping.

But ultimately Morris was, like Ruskin, on the wrong side of history. The Futurists were closer to being correct in their praise of machines. Marinetti's claim that a racing car is more beautiful than the Victory of Samothrace surely speaks directly to contemporary popular taste, with NASCAR now being among the most popular spectator sports in the United States. The Futurists understood that the modern world was a world of active experience rather than a world of passive contemplation or consumption. Their works were themselves often either provocations or hymns in praise of experience. They were ushers, guiding users, into the world of design.

And that world was then, in the early decades of the twentieth century, finally coming into existence. In the chapter "Design and Environment" published in *For A Critique of the Political Economy of the Sign*, Jean Baudrillard claims that our technoculture did not really emerge until the foundation of the Bauhaus. The Bauhaus, he claims,

> institutes the universal semantization of the environment in which everything become the object of a calculus of function and of signification. Total functionality, total semiurgy… This functionality defines itself as a double movement of analysis and rational synthesis of forms (not only industrial, but environmental and social in general). It is a synthesis of form and function, of 'beauty and utility', of art and technology. … It extends the aesthetic to the entire everyday world; at the same

time it is all of technique in the service of everyday life.
(186-7)

With the Bauhaus, our relationship to things changes: functional objects signify with a new fluidity. The whole environment becomes a distinctly new kind of created world: aesthetic and symbolic, functional and abstract all at once. But the transformation inaugurated by that institution was incomplete. The school closed its doors, its teachers dispersed, and the union of art and design, of art and technology eluded other schools.

Two cultures or more

The split between the aesthetic and the scientific is still deeply embedded in the structure of our cultural and educational institutions today. C.P. Snow famously referred to the arts and sciences as "two cultures," suggesting that these two cultures had utterly lost the ability to communicate with one another. Jean-François Lyotard described the same phenomenon as the postmodern condition. In the postmodern condition, according to Lyotard, no single rule holds true in both the qualitative and quantitative research fields.

This division has its roots at the beginning of the modern era, but institutionally, for us, this situation can be traced back to the end of the nineteenth century, when two important changes occurred in the organization of higher education, particularly in the United States. The first change had to do with the separation of liberal arts education from professional or vocational education. The second change concerned the disingenuous alignment of the liberal arts with the quantitative methods and scientistic orientation of the social and hard sciences, primarily through specialization and pseudo-scientific research models.

By aligning themselves with the quantitative methods and scientistic orientation of the social sciences, the qualitative or hermeneutic fields of the Humanities proper hoped to retain some legitimacy in a functionalist or utilitarian culture that only grudgingly retained a place for them. Meanwhile, those schools or programs that edged too close to direct social or financial application were secluded from the liberal arts, either in the form of graduate degrees, as in the case of medical school or law school, or as a "lesser" alternative to liberal arts education, in vocational degrees. This is another story of mutual ambivalence. When information or knowledge presents itself as too close to the world, it is disdained. But it is likewise disdained for being too far from it. Medical school and law school retain a curious allure in our culture as essentially vocational programs in fields endowed with an abstract and transcendent prestige. To be a lawyer or a doctor is not to simply pursue a vocation it is to master the law and life.

These considerations are directly related to the study of art and design in several ways. First, design education has historically been denigrated as a form of vocational education or as a vocational alternative to Fine Art education. Second, design has been affiliated, both internally and externally, with empirical methods of research. Design education has thus stood at a remove from cultural study and it has done so rather willfully.

This dialectical relationship – in which the contemplation of Fine Art equals freedom and the consumption of design equals oppression by market forces – is particularly appealing in the academy, wherein education is often perceived as designed to promote personal liberation. Free subjects cultivate their freedom by contemplating Fine Art, or so the story goes. The contemplation of commodities – the objects of design – seems counter-intuitive, in one sense, and, in a more radical but opposed sense, a dangerous imposition upon the real freedom of the consumer.

Liberal arts education appeals to Fine Art objects to instill the exercise of judgment, the cultivation of taste, which will then be available to the consumer out in the real world. Yet it is all but impossible to imagine a liberal arts education structured around the exercise of critical judgment through the cultivation of taste relevant to the world in which we actually live, to imagine courses focused on design objects – including cuisine – in which students learn to select the things of the world for pleasure and profit. The students – who are in fact already free, at least to some extent, certainly in their own minds – would rebel. Corporations and governments would quiver and quake. For consumption really isn't just a matter of opinion. Taste really can be cultivated and doing so would have vast ramifications on our economy.

But this is an extremely complicated question from an institutional perspective. In our time, the divisions between the arts and sciences, between the cultural and the empirical, the abstract and the applied, have become vastly complicated both inside and outside the walls of the academy. The Humanities fields have suffered an all but terminal loss of prestige and the sciences and social sciences have expanded to consider topics traditionally taken to be the purview of the Humanities fields. Defenders of the Humanities are struggling to find a rationale that resonates with contemporary culture (including their corporatized college administrations). Nevertheless, and in some ways in response to these shifts, several movements are taking place simultaneously.

The hermeneutic disciplines have begun to address the world of design with increasing regularity. Indeed, almost every department on campus has some knowledge worker considering some aspect of design culture. Historians pursue Material

Culture studies. Sociologists and psychologists study consumption. Literature departments have new courses on graphic novels, digital narrativity, and video games, among other design related concerns: from cookbooks to environmentalism and sustainability. Fine Arts programs are more and more interested in visual culture, much of which is graphic design by another name, as well as in the history of the relationship between art and design.

Even the sciences are beginning to be directed toward design studies in specific new ways. To the extent that science is applied science it is often proximate to a field of design or engineering. This is a significant concern for scientists seeking funding for research. Cash strapped universities become design innovation engines when research can be applied. New fields of science – like synthetic biology – are design fields in their own right, and explicitly so.

Moreover, as all of these fields have expanded, they have become increasingly self-aware, and internally complex, encouraging new modes of research, some of which are celebrated as interdisciplinary. Now we have historians and philosophers of science, for example, working in history, philosophy, and in the sciences themselves. Science and Technology Studies (STS) is a field emerging at the intersections of anthropology, philosophy, applied science, and design. (To be truly interdisciplinary these researches must cross the qualitative-quantitative divide, they must be hermeneutic as well as empirical in their methodologies, but this is rare.) My point here is to evoke the vitality and the disorder of these emergent institutional agendas.

And they are not alone. Perhaps even more encouraging than the academic attempts to rethink our approach to objects and making is the range of extra-academic organizations and institutes that have recently appeared. The Rocky Mountain

Institute, the Santa Fe Institute, the Lannan Foundation, Bruce Mau's Institute Without Boundaries, John Thackara's The Doors of Perception conferences, Stewart Brand's Long Now Foundation and his Seminars about Long Term Thinking, John Brockman's The Edge.org, the Ted lectures, the Lift conference, among many other institutes, conferences, seminars, and websites. These are all new centers for research and innovation in design and design thinking. They are operating on the fringes of the academy or in spaces where the academy cannot go, though often building on initial research drawn from the academic context.

John Brockman's TheEdge.org is particularly interesting to me because of Brockman's overarching agenda. Brockman promotes what he calls a "third" culture – in contrast to the two cultures described by C. P. Snow. According to Brockman, the humanities fields have abandoned their historic calling to ask the most searching and revealing questions about the main issues of concern in human life. They have ceded this function to scientists who use empirical methods to investigate these same questions. By doing so, these scientists, at least in Brockman's argument, bring humanism to science. Brockman is a literary agent and self-styled "cultural impresario," who has been instrumental in bringing a great deal of this research to popular consciousness. Stewart Brand and Jared Diamond are among his clients.

Merely adding humanism to science or applied science does not however constitute a revolutionary turn in contemporary thought. More seriously still, it discounts or avoids the genuinely revolutionary turns that have occurred in the Humanities fields over the last forty or so years. And yet these turns have also been discounted by the Humanities fields themselves, which remain distracted by the illusion of total representation in the ethics of multiculturalism. These fields have only grudgingly begun to shift their form and focus from the quest for total representation – through infinite specialization – toward the forces that are actually shaping contemporary culture, like design.

All of these shifts and changes are difficult to summarize. They are not altogether negative. Far from it. The general trend follows increasing development or complexification within disciplines toward an increased awareness of and focus on design, both historically and in contemporary society, without a new overarching appeal to design or design studies as a guiding thread in contemporary education. It is as though everyone were independently working toward the same goal without ever discussing that goal as a group.

Yet the division between the two (or perhaps three) cultures of the academy, between the arts and sciences, is still a serious division and it is a division that can also be found at the center of design studies as an emergent field. Design practitioners tend to pursue empirical research based on a social science model, while design critics, historians, and theorists utilize methods derived from critical cultural studies or at least the philosophy of technology. Many design programs – both historical and practical – are also housed in or with art programs, which favor neither empirical research nor the methods of critical cultural studies. The institutional pairing of art and design – as distinct fields – is also extremely problematic and it cuts to the core of our inquiry.

The Ends of Art

My initial question was perhaps slightly disingenuous. Why do we spend so much time and energy, so much money, personally and culturally, on Fine Art, if design is the primary force shaping our lives? The answer is that we don't. We actually spend far less time and money, far less cultural capital, talking about Fine Art today than might be suspected given the persistent nature of the prestige of Fine Art and its institutions in our culture today. Art has, in other words, become something of a myth in our society, a myth and a sacred cow, endlessly descried and eliminated, that somehow just won't pass away. I would suggest that every new high-profile public investment in our proliferating museums was in fact a case of the emperor's new clothes were it not for the fact that in this case the clothes really do make the man. The buildings themselves matter far more than the things they house.

More and more museums are in fact collecting and showing design, often displaying the objects as if they were Fine Art. But design is not art. And, more importantly, these days art isn't either. The products available in the contemporary Fine Art market no longer serve the social, cultural, or intellectual purposes they did in the modern era and it won't do any us good to pretend that they do.

These are not idle concerns. To question the relationship between Fine Art and design is to question the disposition of energy in our culture. Energy here means not only actual energy – the material basis of wealth – but also intellectual energy, the social system of value. Since the sixteenth century, the Fine Arts have been held up as the bearers of cultural value, carriers of sweetness and light, in the words of Matthew Arnold. But this has never really been the case and it certainly is not the case now.

How can we begin to shift our cultural values – to direct our collective attention to things that actually do impact us – if our eyes remain fixed on outmoded ideological figures?

Part of the problem is that we no longer know what we mean by the word Art. As with all things ideological, the word Art has come to suggest a constant and universal component of human life, even though this suggestion becomes incoherent as soon as anyone examines it closely. If Art refers only to oil paintings, for example, or even just paintings of any kind, it has had a severely restricted history. If Art must be beautiful, its history is even more restricted. If Art refers to the products of a decorative urge, the word is too lacking in specificity to be of any use. Art, for us, certainly for me, refers specifically to the products of the Fine Art tradition. Yet even for many students of art history it is often difficult to remember that the Fine Art tradition is a relatively new phenomenon, historically speaking. It is still more difficult to accept that it may one day pass away as a sphere of significant cultural concern, or, worse yet, that it may already have.

This problem has been a persistent one. As long ago as 1947, André Malraux began his magisterial trilogy on the morphology of forms, *The Voices of Silence*, with a now famous observation: "A Romanesque crucifix was not regarded by its contemporaries as a work of sculpture; nor Cimabue's *Madonna* as a picture. Even Pheidias' *Pallas Athena* was not, primarily, a statue." Put differently, we have the habit of using the word Art and its attendant descriptors – sculpture, picture, etc. – rather too freely. Museums encourage us in this usage as do art history books, particularly textbooks. Such things "estrange" and "transform" (Malraux's words) the works they bring together, erasing their original contexts and turning them into Art.

This gesture extends and fulfills the Hegelian agenda of absolute inclusiveness, of the completion of a world-historical, trans-cultural synthesis of all things, the fabled "global," ency-clopedic perspective. Malraux began his book in 1935, writing under the influence of Walter Benjamin's article on the techno-logical reproduction of art works, just as modern art was itself being codified and collected in museums like the then new Mu-seum of Modern Art in New York. More so than anything else, however, it was technology, including advances in photography and printing that had reinvigorated the Hegelian dream in the age of totalitarianisms.

In our time even more so than in Malraux's this problem has become acute. The "new" academic textbooks in Art History and in the Humanities have been expanded beyond their tradi-tional forms to include Art from the non-Western world even though the cultural production of that world falls decidedly outside the history of the Fine Art tradition. The forms may in some cases be familiar – paintings, statues, etc. – but the social functions are decidedly different, as are the cultural contexts and processes that produced these creations. It is unsurprising that these differences might too easily be elided in our cultural quest for a synthesis born of similarities. Even as we attempt to respect difference, by representing "different" things, we erase that very difference by making all of these different things the same, by turning all cultural production into what we in the global West call Art. In order to end cultural imperialism we must stop imposing our cultural categories on objects produced by other cultures both historically and in our own times. Fine Art is, in short, a distinctly Western phenomenon.

Moreover, these textbooks and the discipline they represent haven't quite been able to get around the notion that the Fine Art tradition – and I shouldn't have to say Modern Western Fine Art tradition, for there is no other – might in fact have reached its end. To suggest that art is everywhere, all the time, is to suggest that it cannot or could not have come to an end. But this is to say nothing of the cultural institution of Fine Art. Manifestly the products of the Fine Art tradition no longer function as significant forms of cultural expressiveness and critical self-reflection. This situation is of course complicated by the fact that the Fine Art tradition brought this state upon itself through the internal refinement and circumscription of its forms and effects.

By suggesting that the Fine Art tradition has reached its end I am merely echoing the very diverse views of several prominent academic art critics, Hans Belting, Donald Kuspit, Arthur Danto, and Johanna Drucker perhaps most notably. Indeed, the end of art has become even more prominent than the death of god as a field of morbid but persistent speculation. The persistence of this speculation is of course the root paradox currently under consideration. It is clearly visible in most of these critical approaches to the end of art. Each critic observes, in his or her own fashion, with his or her own distinct arguments, the end of art, only to resurrect it with some *deus ex machina* argument in the final chapters. Yes, the critic intones, the tradition as we knew and loved it has come to an end, but this does not mean that Art is dead, no, it simply means that Art serves a new and distinct, *even more interesting* function in contemporary society (Danto, *After the End of Art*), or that a few rogue artists are just now rediscovering the very roots of the form in new art (Kuspit, *The End of Art*; Johanna Drucker, *Sweet Dreams*).

Another group of texts also testifies to the same social fact from a very different direction. These are critical writings of a less theoretical, more journalistic bent that have spent the last decade and more skewering contemporary art and the contemporary art market, books as diverse as James Gardner's *Culture or Trash*, Anthony Haden-Guest's *True Colors*, Matthew Collings' *It Hurts*, and Julian Stallabrass' *Art Incorporated*, among many

many others, and these are just the books. Newspaper and other critics continue the effort in less persistent forms. Again and again New York Times art critics observe the empty aegis of contemporary Fine Art under the sway of commerce and fashion, and they as a group often actually seem to like contemporary art. But they write like betrayed believers, disappointed in their god. Much of the material in these books and articles might be considered anecdotal in hindsight, evidencing the emptiness of particular artists rather than of the cultural form itself, but as chronicles they are profoundly wearying.

This is not the place to engage with all of the anecdotes and arguments presented in all of these books. Their existence alone might satisfy some as to the validity of the observation that something is rotten in the art market. Collectively these writers keep throwing every notion they have into the pot without concern for the broader cultural consistency of their logic. The only points of commonality seem to be that Fine Art has changed profoundly from its historic form and that Fine Art continues to be produced. In other words, everything has changed and nothing has changed. I'd like to sketch this shift very briefly so that thereafter we might better understand the relationship between art and design.

The Fine Art of communication

In the 1640s, a group of *kloveniers*, a harquebusier shooting militia in Amsterdam, commemorated its actions in the recent wars with a series of large scale group portraits, the most memorable of which, from the perspective of hindsight, was by Rembrandt van Rijn. Rembrandt's *The Night Watch* depicts Banning Cocq and his lieutenant, Willem van Ruytenburgh, with sixteen militia men welcoming Maria de' Medici's daughter, Henrietta

Maria, a Catholic queen fleeing Anglican England and the tide of revolution, to Amsterdam. A crowded dramatic orgy of light and darkness, of color and conflicting line, *The Night Watch* is an eminently *social* painting. It depicts real people doing a real thing in a real – if dramatically intensified, even claustrophobic – space. And it was originally hung as it was meant to be in a very public place, the *kloveniers groote sael* being grand enough to be rented by the city for festive occasions when not in use by its members. The individuals depicted in the painting paid, on a two-tiered scale, to have their images included in it. And they were painted as a group. Significantly, the deposed queen is herself the most diminutive figure in the painting. Ostensibly the honored quest of the city, she is almost an afterthought buried in the martial display. The painting, in other words, and in almost every way, harkens the new democratic world order. It is a painting of the people for the people, paid for by the people, and it is impossible to imagine anything like it happening today.

Three hundred or so years later, a Spanish painter living in Paris, Pablo Picasso, stretched an enormous canvas, twenty six feet by twelve, in his new studio on the rue des Grands-Augustins. The studio walls themselves dripped with the history of painting: Balzac had set his famous story *Chef-d'oeuvre inconnu* in that building a century before. But Picasso's new work would be anything but unknown. He was then painting an outraged response to a social crisis, the civil war that then gripped his native land. In particular, he was painting in protest against the bombing of the city of Guernica in northern Spain by the German Luftwaffe, who were fighting on the side of the Spanish Fascists commanded by Franco. On the night of April 26th 1937, incendiary and high-explosive bombs killed 1,654 and wounded 889 civilians in a town of roughly 7,000. Picasso worked for weeks on sketches and to complete the canvas which came to be commissioned by the Spanish Republican government for the *Exposition Internationale des Arts et Techniques dans la Vie Moderne*, part of the World's Fair in Paris.

In shades of grey and black, the painting itself is at once symbolic and shockingly visceral. A screaming mother carries the corpse of her dead child into the viewer's line of sight. The dismembered fragments of a soldier litter the ground, his sword broken. A bull bellows, wide-eyed. A horse is slaughtered in agony. Shocked spectators look up from below and down from above; mouths agape, they cry to the sky. An electric bulb burns as an enormous interrogating eye: less the vision of justice than the sight of a torturer. The symbolic forms are ancient and modern at once, Mediterranean, solar and secular simultaneously. The distorted forms of Picasso's creation were profoundly appropriate to his subject matter. No one could escape his meaning.

In 1939, the painting moved to New York, to the then relatively new Museum of Modern Art, though it traveled extensively over the next few decades representing several things at once: the atrocity of war, the Spanish Republican cause, the evils of Fascism, and the genius of Picasso. Though the painting explicitly condemned the repressive violence of his regime, Franco sought to have it sent to Spain toward the end of his life. Picasso for his part blocked any such action, stipulating even in his will that the painting should not travel to Spain until Spain was again a republic, with democratic social institutions. Even at the end of the 1970s, after Picasso's death, after Franco's death two years later, and after the transformation of the Spanish state, the Museum of Modern Art was still reluctant to give up its treasure. In 1981, they did, sending the painting to the Prado in Madrid. Later it would be transferred to a specially designed space in the nearby Museo Nacional Centro de Arte Reina Sofía.

As with Rembrandt's *Night Watch*, it is all but impossible to imagine a contemporary work creating such a furor and compelling such interest, internationally, either today or over so many decades. Like *The Night Watch*, *Guernica* is in many ways a work of public art. Though it is distinctly abstract and symbolic rather than realistically representational, and though it was painted by an individual painter following his lights rather by a painter following the dictates of his patrons, it is a work of public art. Picasso painted it in the idiom of his day – an idiom he helped invent – to say something to the people of his time about a significant communal event, something that he thought was significant to the international community and that had happened within or rather *to* a small community in Spain. The painting was created for a public exhibition rather than for a gallery space or for exhibition in a home. From its inception it had a public destiny rather than a private one. It is a work that challenges the purposes of the museum in which it is on display simply through the powerful directness of its politicized speech. It belongs in the street, wherever state violence threatens civil liberty.

Picasso wasn't alone in painting very public works in the 1930s. It was an age of ideologies, and ideologies require advertisement. Hitler, Stalin and Mussolini all invested in public art and so did Franklin Delano Roosevelt. The Works Progress Administration sponsored a vast Federal Art Project beginning in 1935, commissioning all manner of murals, sculptures, and easel paintings. The Farm Security Administration commissioned photographers and writers to document the plight of the nation's rural poor. These federal projects only helped fuel an agenda that the artists themselves were already pursuing. Painters as different as Thomas Hart Benton and Ben Shahn shared a concern for the common good. Benton's murals in particular sought to tell the tale of America, or at least one version of it, to

Americans. The Federal Art Project commissioned murals like these all over the country. The paintings might not all be great art but they speak more or less directly to people about things that matter to them. I say speak because these paintings continue to and because murals continue to be executed in a style inspired if not by Benton then by Mexican masters of the form like Diego Rivera. Rivera's works typically harness a symbolic power that is distinctly absent from Benton's.

I have chosen these examples purposefully. Rembrandt, Picasso, Benton, and Rivera represent a very diverse group of painters both in terms of historical periods, national affiliation and style. Their works cannot be confused. But across this diversity they share a common concern for communication and a common mission of motivating their viewers with emotion. They speak to their viewers through the medium of paint and they offer those viewers the opportunity to reflect on themselves by reflecting on their art works. The pleasures and challenges of paintings, and of works of art in general, are manifold. They are always and to varying degrees both physical and intellectual, and, in the nexus between these two, emotional. Or at least they were.

The art of the nineteen thirties was perhaps the last art that a truly broad cross-section of the public actually enjoyed in common. This is not a statement about the quality of the art produced since then nor about the quality of the public, in the sense of generalized aesthetic awareness, but rather a statement about the social function of art. After the nineteen thirties, Fine Art and the public drifted further and further apart, without any particular concern for one another. Beyond the confines of the academy, beyond the gallery districts in New York, the vast amorphous public still loves Art from that and prior eras and oddly even still claims to be radical by professing a love for abstraction.

Contemporary Fine Artists are likely to fault the previous few paragraphs for being nostalgic, for lamenting the loss of something that had real and recognizable limits. Undoubtedly this is true, but it is not my only point.

Marcel Duchamp once quipped that museum visitors should have to pass a test prior to admittance. Art, he suggested, is like any other specialized field and should be treated as such. Simply put, not everyone knows everything about art, nor is art immediately available to all spectators. The relativist notion that every individual is entitled to his or her own opinion about everything, and about art in particular, is only partially true and significantly avoids the crucial question. Do these individuals have any idea what they are talking about? Do they have the tools – analytical, informational – to form an accurate and just opinion about the topic at hand? Duchamp is suggesting that we should have the good taste to admit that we often don't. In a specialized culture it is important to delegate. Not everyone *should* attempt to form an opinion about everything. We simply can't.

If Duchamp is right, we shouldn't worry about things that don't concern to us, in the fullest sense of the word concern. And of course most of us don't. How many Americans today might be able to name a contemporary artist working in the Fine Art tradition or identify one of that artist's works? I am not suggesting that we don't need to hone our aesthetic senses. I think we do. We just don't need to worry so much about Fine Art. After all, designers make most of the things we see every day. We – all of us – cut our aesthetic teeth on design, not on Fine Art.

Before we turn more directly to the question of design, we might look at what I'll call the internal erosion of the tradition of Fine Art. The Fine Art tradition and the public didn't just drift apart. The Fine Art tradition evolved in such a way as to erode the basis of broad public interest in it. That it did so in an era in which the design arts attained their own apotheosis is not entirely ironic.

Why bother to continue talking about the Fine Art tradition at this point? Primarily so that we can understand what happened to it and secondarily so that we can understand what we've both lost and gained. The second of these points is obviously more significant, particularly as we begin to try to understand what the design arts are in fact doing for us. A tertiary point will also haunt our schema. As noted previously, several prominent design writers persistently insist that design objects can be compared to Fine Art, and that the methods of art criticism might be appropriate to design writing. By illustrating the very significant differences between the social institutions of Fine Art and design, I hope to dissuade these writers from this purpose. This in mind, a thumb-nail sketch: a history of movements in late modern art in six familiar steps: Dada, Abstract Expressionism, Neo-Dada, Pop Art, Minimalism and everything after.

The internal erosion of the Fine Art tradition

Art has been dead or dying for a long time. Almost one hundred years ago, at the Cabaret Voltaire in Zurich in 1916, Hugo Ball, Emmy Hennings, Richard Huelsenbeck, Tristan Tzara, Hans Arp, Sophie Tauber, Marcel Janco, and some others, put a bullet in the Fine Art tradition as a vehicle of so-called Enlightened ideals, a conveyor of sweetness and light. They wore masks, danced unchoreographed dances, and sang incomprehensible songs, beat drums. They did several things simultaneously, everything all at once. Dada began as an anti-war movement but it quickly progressed into a protest against everything that had caused the war as well: every faith, every economic interest, every ideal, beauty or otherwise. If art works led to war, the Dadaists would make anti-art: every work designed as an undoing, a *un*-work. Hugo Ball in particular pursued a rather thorough critique of Western civilization in his book, *Critique of the German Intelligentsia*, and in his journals, later published as *Flight Out of Time*. If Dada was a savage attack on civilization, it was also an equally savage attack on the subject of that civilization: modern man. And it wasn't easy: "I sometimes feel as if I were being torn apart and beaten limb by limb," Ball wrote, though he himself was doing the beating. In an interview in 1975, the French philosopher Henri Lefebvre characterized Zurich Dada as the "radical negation" modernity had been carrying within itself from its inception. Dada was the hidden face, the negative image, the contradiction of modernity. Dada rejected the ground, purpose, and methods of the Fine Art tradition. It cast everything about it into doubt.

Of course it couldn't last. Dada wasn't intended to endure nor was it intended to lead to anything else. But it was nevertheless strange, uncanny even, how quickly everyone just picked up the pieces and moved on, almost as if nothing had happened, as if they hadn't learned anything at all. Richard Huelsenbeck went back to Germany at the end of the war and became a committed political artist under the banner of a rejuvenated Dada spirit. In Zurich, Dada had known nothing of commitment: commitment led to war. Tristan Tzara, for his part, went on to Paris where he became an aesthetic agitator for a few years. But Dada couldn't really be reduced to a catalogue of stylistic effects. It was negation or it was nothing at all. Within a few years, André Breton stole the show for his nascent Surrealist movement. Hugo Ball retired to Italy to write books about Christian culture – his adventures in negativity had made him a mystic.

Since then Dada has been rediscovered many times. Robert Motherwell edited and published an anthology of writings by

Dada painters and poets in 1951, just as Abstract Expression-ism reached the height of its ascendancy. Robert Rauschenberg would soon be branded neo-dada for specious reasons. Fluxus and the other performance artists of the 1960s would carry the flame, in their way, for a while, then punk rock would carry it to its grave. But the claim at the core of it – the big No – has not changed: The Fine Art tradition is a tradition of fraud: repre-sentation is just a lie. The myth of the "autonomous individual," dismantled by Nietzsche and Freud, unmasked at the Caba-ret Voltaire, is a chimera used to manipulate the unsuspecting masses. Self= stooge. We are fools to forget it.

One can forgive Picasso and his generation for missing the memo. They were already on the scene when the Dadaists began their show. The stage itself started to crack with the next genera-tion. Jackson Pollock was only four when Huelsenbeck started beating his drum but no small part of Pollock's destructive ener-gy would be derived from the potentiality of Dada (via Surrealist experiments with automatism and chance). After Dada, any-thing is possible. After Dada, nothing really matters, the whole set up was hanging by a thread.

Pollock took Picasso's deconstructed biomorphic forms, Thomas Hart Benton's energetic sinuous lines, and the size and ambition of the Mexican muralists, injected evidence of his process, psychological and otherwise, and turned the tradi-tion resolutely toward a new kind of free abstraction. Pollock's work carries on a dialogue with the tradition, and hence is part of the tradition, but it also made a profound step beyond what went before him. He did not make the leap entirely alone but for our limited purposes his name can stand-in for Abstract Ex-pressionism. Unencumbered by an image, by representation, Pollock's works can be profoundly emotional in a raw, physi-cal way. Purely formal, they cannot be said to have content in any previously appropriate sense of this term. They don't show us anything; rather they take our eyes on a trip. They give us a chance to see, to follow colors and lines, contrasts, coils and confusion, reconciled and unfinished at once. An unresolved swarm of color, they cannot quite be called complete or incomplete. Alongside the occasionally visible hand-prints and ephemera impacted into the paint, this element of incompletion signals the process involved in creating one of these works. Pollock claimed his large format works anticipated the art of the future which he believed would be environmental, what McLuhan would have called immersive, what I understand as the province of design.

From Picasso to Pollock, the Fine Art tradition lost representation, which is also to say that it exposed the problem of culture beyond representation. It gained respect for the residue of process in the work but it lost its most basic means of connecting with its public. (Feeling is actually primary but, let's face it, most people don't know how to feel: they prefer to see with their minds, they look for something they recognize and find beauty there.) Some of the other abstract expressionists hedged their bets. Willem de Kooning pushed at the limits of representation, twisting, torturing, exaggerating and fracturing images rather than just simply letting them go. Barnett Newman gave his works evocative titles and "explained" them with reference to religious stories and symbols. Sometimes his stories were better than others, even better than the paintings. But stories never really adhere to a visual work unless they are clearly visible within it. They are a dangerous supplement: they undermine the validity of the thing they are attempting to prop up. Is the meaning of the work in the story or is it in the work? Why should I bother to look if I have to know something that I don't know in order to see? This problem would only become more acute as the tradition continued to erode.

Robert Rauschenberg took the next step. He famously rejected the Ab-Ex aesthetic as essentially bullying. He faulted Pollock and his cohort for taking their emotions on parade and for failing to give the viewer anything to do or think about other than wallow in the creator's glory. Rauschenberg managed to create works that would remain open to many interpretations; interpretations that each viewer would have to supply independently. Pollock's paintings did not represent anything and Rauschenberg's works wouldn't either. But Rauschenberg would reveal the process of signification at work in his pieces. He painted the quilt and pillow from his actual bed and called it *Bed*, thereby shaking the word loose from complacent usage. Is *Bed* a painting of a bed or a painted bed? Is the work still a bed if it is a painted bed? Is it still private if it is public? Rauschenberg's early works turned reality into a spectacle by including real photographs and cast-off cultural detritus – stuffed birds, pillows, tires – into them. Gradually Rauschenberg began to explore new technologies of image reproduction and manufacture – pioneering new printing processes among other things. By the early 1960s his works had also begun to include all manner of found images: from technologically reproduced elements from the Fine Art tradition to personal photographs to magazine and newspaper clippings to advertisements and signage. The last four of these categories are of course the products of graphic design, which had attained a new social prominence in Rauschenberg's lifetime. It is unsurprising that an artist interested in social processes of signification should be interested in graphic design. It is surprising that such an artist might not dabble in design himself.

Rauschenberg's combines and silkscreen works aren't meant to be beautiful. To call them beautiful is to offer an interpretation of them, to settle them once and for all. Rather, they exist to offer each viewer a field of investigation, selected and arranged by Rauschenberg to be sure, but left open to an interrogation that must be renewed with each glance. This openness stands in direct opposition to the Abstract Expressionist aesthetic and it can be understood either positively or negatively. Positively, Rauschenberg liberated Fine Art from the tyranny of the expressive ego just as Pollock liberated it from the demands of representation. Negatively, Rauschenberg dispensed with the last vestige of communication shared between artist and viewer. Rauschenberg's works don't offer us anything in particular to see, feel, or think, they are perhaps *too* open to interpretation. Why should we bother to look at them? This openness might be interpreted positively, as a Zen-inspired approach to the world, or negatively as nihilism, void of meaning.

Andy Warhol stepped into that void. He famously wanted to become a machine. His work can be understood as the dialectical unfolding of this desire. If in the beginning he put his training as a commercial illustrator to work by personally painting pictures by hand, he nevertheless took a first step toward his goal by effectively eliminating subject matter: he painted hegemonic images from the new visual ecology, which is to say from the worlds of media and design. This still seemed too personal, so he took another step: he serialized the images, draining them of whatever limited uniqueness they might still have possessed. This too was too personal so he traded his brushes for silkscreens. Then he let other people run the prints. He called his studio a factory and encouraged members of his entourage to make his art for him. He began to transition into film and recordings, letting technology take over. He designed record covers. Originally trained and employed as a graphic artist, he entered the realm of Fine Art by refusing the creative responsibility of the graphic artist, a refusal he effected by copying graphic art rather than creating it. Here again the work is not meant to be beautiful nor evocative nor emotional nor communicative. It creates a perfect void in the tradition.

Generally speaking, Pop Art in America, Warhol and beyond, derives from design. It may change the scale of a piece or it may change its texture but it derives from design. It may have done this in order to make us think about the process and role of signification in our lives. It may have done this as a daring and rebellious gesture, conflating high culture and low culture in some then new (1960s) way. It's hard to see such gestures as particularly rebellious from our historical perspective. I can explain it as such if pressed, but I don't really feel the rebellion in my bones the way I do when I read Hugo Ball's writings or flip through a catalog of Dada works. Ultimately, for me, it comes down to the fact that Pop Art just doesn't give me much to do, think, or feel. A giant clothespin in a city park is still a clothespin, it is just less interesting, less motivated.

Minimalism pushed this problem just a little bit further into the void. Minimalism and Pop art both confront the challenge of design but they do so in opposed ways. Pop Art embraces design, and reifies it as art. Minimalism attempts to work around it, by making what we might call "not design". Frank Stella's dictum "what you see is what you see" or Donald Judd's suggestion that his objects lack any significance beyond what is literally there tell only half the story; for minimalism, like design, begins as a dialogue with materials. Whereas designers attempt to create images and objects that will activate as many economies of meaning as possible and thereby motivate involvement (consumption being only one model of this), minimalists strive to separate their work from every economy save one, that of the Fine Art tradition. Minimalist art is thus best understood by negation: it is not representational, not symbolic, not iconic, not personal, not expressive, not decorative, not ornamental, not beautiful, not sensuous (for its own sake), not conceptual (not yet), and, most of all, not functional. Minimalism is in short not any of the things that art and design used to be. Yet minimalist masters (!) must often walk the tensed line between art and design. Already in the 1960s, Donald Judd had begun using commercial manufacturers to make his pieces, just as a furniture designer would. Later he would actually start designing furniture.

Postart

After Pop and Minimalism, the Fine Art tradition had essentially emptied itself out and, perhaps more importantly, come to function only in reaction to the world of design. Allan Kaprow suggested more or less this same thing already in the 1960s. It took other critics another twenty or even thirty years to catch up with him and, obviously, the public still haven't caught up. Art goes on. Or something like it does. Donald Kuspit calls it "postart" in *The End of Art*. We might just call it contemporary art. After the end, anything goes, at least after a fashion. Anything goes so long as it is in fact *something*. Contemporary art is almost immeasurably diverse in form, content, and orientation. But this diversity is often only apparent, superficial even. Fundamentally deprived, contemporary art proposes itself as a collection of singularities, of radically compartmentalized gestures of meaning-making. It appears heroic only against the backdrop of its devastated field: it seems miraculous that anything could be meaningful after the end and yet each contemporary art object proposes itself as meaningful in some unique way. An object may not be pretty but it shows process. It may not be original but this is its "critique" of the system. It may not be powerful on its own but it is political and derives interest from the larger social debate about race or gender identities (the class struggle having disappeared from contemporary aesthetic consciousness). As a field of singularities, contemporary art lends itself to the proliferation of mini-movements and styles. Detached from the grand tradition, micro-traditions spring up and pass away at any point of intersection: material, geographical, temporal, ideological, political. Any logic suffices for a curator.

A few years ago, Johanna Drucker mounted a vigorous defense of contemporary art in her book *Sweet Dreams*. She began with a vaguely Aristotlean notion that criticism should follow creativity. Rather than claiming that contemporary art is not in fact art, as in the postart argument, the critic should, she claims, assume that contemporary art is actually art and then try to understand it. Artists are supposed to be smarter or more insightful than the rest of us, after all, or so the story goes.

Most contemporary art criticism, she argues, is beholden to a tradition of cultural critique that no longer applies to contemporary art. If the critical model no longer fits the art, the critical model must change, or so she claims. Her argument is reminiscent in an interesting way of the Dalai Lama's assertion that Buddhism must adapt itself to the claims of science: when science and Buddhism disagree, Buddhism must change. But of course Drucker is talking about Fine Art rather than about science. The purpose of science is to make defensible claims about the nature of our physical world. The purpose of art is much more difficult to define.

Contemporary art, in her reading, is an art of complicity and ambiguity. By complicit she means that contemporary art replicates many of the forms and assumptions of contemporary culture – which often means consumer culture, design culture – without attempting to transform those positions or to isolate itself from them. Populist, racist, sexist, what have you, the art is justifiable as art. Hence, in a way, its ambiguity. It is impossible to say whether the replicated form or structure is being indicted or affirmed. I would say that contemporary art simply is what it is … but it isn't – it's art.

Ambiguity in contemporary art is akin to but the inverse of communication in modern art. Great modern art communicates many things all at once and it does so in the form of an open question, a field of potentiality open to our senses and imagination, and thus to our aesthetic judgment. Contemporary art on the other hand often conveys its ambiguity in one specific act. The specificity of contemporary art is significant: without it the art could not demonstrate its connection to the tradition or to culture or to anything else and hence its status as art. Contemporary art is thus often clever rather than creative (in the fullest sense of this term), the pointed but ambiguous modification of one existent image, idea, or gesture. Very often this singular image, idea or gesture is obscure upon our first encounter with the object. The object in other words does not contain enough information to speak on its own. We need to know something about the artist or about something else to "decode" the work. Only after we've decoded it does the work offer itself to interpretation. It is important that we not mistake this reticence for difficulty. Difficult art tells us too much, reticent art doesn't tell us enough. I would say that the appeal of reticent or ambiguous works is a matter of taste though technically it isn't. The exercise of taste requires an act of judgment and this kind of art denies, through impoverishment, our capacity to form judgments about it. We can only stand before it waiting for the artist or curator or some informed critic to tell us what we need to know to unlock the work. Only then will we begin to understand just how clever the work really is.

At its best, the art world that appears in Drucker's account parallels our own world, which leaves me to wonder why I should bother with it when the world itself is closer to hand. At its worst, that art world is substantially less interesting than our world. However impressed we may be with some of its confections, we often lower our expectations when we encounter them. We are pleased that art objects exist more so than pleased by the objects themselves. In general, the objects of the art world are less thoughtfully articulated, less carefully crafted, less communicative, less indicative of anything, less moving, and, however complicit they may be, they are nevertheless set apart from our world, drifting free from the dirty business of life. By our world, I mean the world of design.

Art and design, again

Manifestly, and as I have already observed, the worlds of art and design have had a contentious relationship since the Fine Arts managed to separate themselves from design some four hundred or so years ago. Both are arts of making, or *poiesis*; skills of creation, of delineation or measurement, of setting things apart from one another through shaping. Proximate in a dialectical way, the two cannot quite be defined separately from one another. Indeed, for much of their entwined history, the difference between art and design has been one of degree rather than kind. For graphic artists, the *kind* of activity has been similar if not in fact the same as for Fine Artists, only the degree to which the artist has been beholden to a particular client, community or concern has changed.

This is significant. Very often in our discussions of art and design we suggest that the difference between the two types of making is inherent in and obviously related to the nature of the completed object, the painting or the poster, for example. We claim that the Fine Art object is fine because its nature is such that it has detached itself, by internal means, from any economy of passionate interest or concern. In other words, Pop art is Pop *art* because it has extracted the sign that is its content from the world of commerce and freed it for our dispassionate contemplation. It has been aided in this task by the art institution, by galleries, museums, and critics whose function is to isolate objects both from one another and from our world. By offering us this mode of contemplation, Fine Art offers us a unique means of access to ourselves as autonomous individuals delivered from the petty concerns and involvements of our day. We both lose ourselves and find ourselves in the contemplation of Fine Art, or so the story goes.

It's a nice story but it has only occasionally been true. From its origins through the 1930s, Fine Art obeyed a communicative necessity that grounded its quest for autonomy in recognizable forms. It cast itself into the wide chasm between these two agendas. Michelangelo famously painted in service to his Pope, under the dictates of theological advisors. He gave form to ideological messages just as any designer would. Fine Art, in other words and for good or ill, has always been art in the service of ideology. Even Kandinsky's abstract art serviced his theosophical worldview.

The autonomy of the object ultimately has little to do with the autonomy of the maker or vice versa. To think otherwise has been a late modern mistake. Fine Artists fulfill commissions just as designers do. The fabled autonomy of the object is rooted in the physiology of perception. Human beings are inveterate idol makers. Physiologically isolated, biologically fragile, existentially alone, we are hungry for meaning and natural discriminators. This makes us easy prey for psycho-pomps and confidence men, for any trickster with a pedestal to sell.

This is particularly ironic given the essentially totalizing motives of the museum industry. Museums simultaneously isolate and collate, gathering objects and dispersing them at once. They improve our perception in this way, creating an ordered, often chronological, cosmos from a disordered group of things. But to mistake this cosmos for reality is to put the cart before the horse, ideologically speaking.

The discourses of Fine Art and design have, of course, fallen prey to this false consciousness. In part because design critics and historians so frequently come from among the ranks of art critics and historians, because, in other words, they share the same basic education in the arts, the two share a narrative about Fine Art and design: in this narrative, Fine Artists create profoundly original cultural forms which are then popularized by designers. Fine Artists, in short, are meaning-makers, designers are meaning-copiers; Artists are originators, designers disseminators, popularizers. There may very well have been cases in which this did happen, but no story like this is ever absolutely hegemonic and the histories of these two forms are so intertwined that it will be impossible to sort the situation out completely.

Art or design

Shifting this topic only slightly, we might observe that many of the great movements in modern art were actually movements in modern design. This is not to say that they were *also* movements in modern design but rather that they were movements in design first and foremost. Our retrospective gaze has often neutered these movements, made them museum-worthy. Even our design histories tend to do the same thing.

From this perspective, movements in modern design are movements that, each in its own way, each for its own reasons, attempt to change everyday life. These movements have often been reactions against the perceived soullessness of industrial manufacturing. In the nineteenth century, they included the Arts and Crafts movement in England, Art Nouveau in France, Jungendstil in Germany; then, in the early twentieth: Futurism, Dada, Surrealism, Suprematism, Constructivism, Purism, the Bauhaus. These are only the most well known. These movements do not circumscribe every movement within modern art, only several very well known movements within it.

There is a dialectic to these movements as well. The first generation – in the nineteenth century – reacted against industrial manufacturing by proposing a return to artisanal production or something like it. The second generation – that of the early twentieth century – embraced industrial production and attempted to refine its processes and purposes through heightened rationalization. Simultaneously, a counter-tendency appeared in the form of anti-art, irrationalism, and the valorization of the non-objective (Malevich).

By the 1950s, these tendencies had recovered from the two-fold catastrophe of economic depression and war, regrouped and again squared off against one another. Modern design had come into its own through the rationalization of its means in the "International Style" and with the aide of the then emergent field of Cybernetics (Norbert Weiner). But counter-tendencies appeared in the Black Mountain School in North Carolina (where Charles Olson replaced Joseph Albers), in Asger Jorn's New Imaginist Bauhaus, and in the Independent Group in London, among many groups. These counter-tendencies injected emotion, imagination, and chance into the rationalized cybernetic field. They rejected the totalizing tendency of modern art and design.

The Independent Group is particularly compelling for our purposes in that it brought together many constituencies, however briefly. Associated with the Institute of Contemporary Arts in London from 1952 to 1955, the Group included architects, sculptors, painters and other visual artists, along with critics, Reyner Banham most notably. As with the other counter-tendencies in high modernism, the Group endeavored to undermine the hegemonic status of high modern art *and* design. British Pop Art, like that of Richard Hamilton and Eduardo Paolozzi, emerged from the Group as did Peter and Alison Smithson's New Brutalist architecture. The Independent Group served as a kind of a think tank on contemporary culture. At once creative and critical, it defined problems and proposed solutions. It *studied* culture, high and low, art and design, and also staged important shows and forged creative advances in all of these areas. This is surely a model for our own endeavors.

Fifty years later, design education largely lacks a critical component and art education is struggling in its ambivalent relationship to design. But how much of contemporary art owes its life to design? Walking through galleries our gaze encounters post-pop images derived from the design fields, art that either derives from or verges on illustration, paintings that recall narrative forms of graphic art; or objects derivative of the process-oriented craft tradition, but made useless.

We might conclude these reflections on the dialectics of art and design with another quip from Marcel Duchamp: There is no solution because there is no problem. The paradigm shifted out from under the traditional discourses of art and design. Artists and designers continue to carry on, respecting the hierarchy that has guided their world since the early industrial era, but we the people live differently. We use things differently. We live in a world beyond representation, a culture created by design.

Beyond Representation

We no longer live in a world predominately organized by structures or technologies of representation, either metaphorically or in fact. We certainly do not live in a world organized primarily by the types of images and texts that are often valorized in our discourses about ourselves, which is to say the languages of literature, visual art, or even visual culture.

We are however surrounded by representations, even drowning in them. Our world is saturated with images and information. We obviously still need to improve our ability to interpret and create them. But take another look at the images and texts around us. Graphic designers created most of the images and texts that we encounter on a daily basis. And these images are in fact assemblages of images and texts rather than either texts or images created or encountered in isolation. These assemblages might include texts and photographs or illustrations, drawings, even paintings. They might appear on billboards or posters, in magazines or newspapers, even in books, though fewer and fewer of the books produced and sold today can be counted as literature, even of the popular kind. As noted before, it was fully one hundred years ago that the French poet Guillaume Apollinaire proclaimed handbills, catalogues and posters the poetry of his times in *Zone*. Now even the moving images that splash across our screens – our televisions and computers, our iPods, iPads and iPhones – owe much of their vitality to the creativity of designers, who work with and through client constraints and often as part of teams. With all this in mind, once again, why do we spend so much time talking about art and literature, or even film, when these other forms of cultural production clearly dominate our lives?

Setting the confusion between art and advertising aside for the moment, we should also notice that these structures and technologies of image transmission, presentation, and memory are only a part of our world and aren't even the most pervasive part. They aren't the most pervasive part – the determinative element – because they do not determine their own platforms and contexts of delivery. Images and texts circulate in and on a world created by other design disciplines. Urban planners map our city streets, architects build our buildings, landscape architects reintegrate our cities into nature and nature into our cities, graphic designers label our environment with signs telling us where we are, showing us how to reach our destination, and marking our places and spaces. Fashion designers make our clothes, industrial designers make our objects – our toothbrushes and toasters, our tables and chairs – and interior designers help us arrange these things in a functional and pleasant way. Graphic designers design the books, newspapers, and websites that we read. We live in a world created by designers. But beyond a superficial level, we don't really think about it, we don't talk about it, and we don't even seem to know how to talk about it.

Never have human beings controlled so much of our environment as completely as we do now. Never have we been able to select from so wide a variety of sources for materials and goods, so rich and wide a variety of things in our lives. Once upon a time cities and neighborhoods grew over centuries, through the combined efforts of generations upon generations of inhabitants. Now they can be created by a small team of developers working with a single architect in a matter of months. Suburbs sprawl like mushrooms overnight and fade as fast as last year's clothes. Conspicuous consumption can't be confined to the leisure class; there's something in it for everyone, and living without is not an option. Our only real choice is to opt *in* with as much wisdom and information as we can. In order to do that we need to have a better sense of the role design decisions play in shaping our lives.

One challenge is presented by the fact that it's difficult for us to conceive of design as an isolated part or element of our world. Design describes the process of engagement that created the entirety of the way that we live. Representations can be isolated from the whole, categorized, and organized: understood apart. But design can't. It's too diffuse, too pervasive and it is also never quite fully present. Design decisions can of course be isolated, one from another, but design as a total context and process consists of so many decisions and elements that our minds quickly recoil before its complexity. Design is not one thing, it is a world within which we live, and, I suspect, many of us would rather not think about it.

The shift from a culture of representation to a culture of design matters for several reasons. To understand it we need to understand what the culture of representation was, where it came from, and where it went.

Representations – art and literature, for example – served and in some ways continue to serve significant personal and social functions. They formed a field apart from the world, a corner of calm amidst the chaos in which an individual might contemplate him or herself and his or her world. Representations were relays and delays for self and society, a pause in presence. And they were much more than that. Collected and collated they were consciousness congealed, history packed in ice, personal and communal memory. Structures and technologies of representation are also structures and technologies of selfhood and society, with their attendant social institutions: structures of government, libraries, museums, and schools structured as repositories of representations. The end of the age of representation signals the end of a kind of reflexive subjectivity as it has been conceived in the West since Augustine's *Confessions*. Obviously this does not mean that people – that is, individuals – will cease to exist. We won't. Only that our individual and social discourse about ourselves, our means of thinking about ourselves, of interacting with ourselves, indeed of being ourselves, will change. And of course I am arguing that it already has. Michel Foucault said the same thing thirty years ago in his writings and lectures about "technologies of the self."

Structures and technologies of representation obviously still exist and will continue to. New ones will continue to be invented. But these technologies have been subsumed by the waters of a more powerful flood flowing from the fount of design. Design creates the underlying and overarching structures, the space and horizon within and against which we live. And the design arts are not arts of representation. They use or incorporate representations but they cannot be confined or isolated in the same way that representations are designed to be. This is one reason they are so difficult to see, appreciate, and discuss.

By technologies of representation, I am primarily referring to certain types of communications media, though the phrase can also reference styles of thought organized around mental representations among many other structures of thought and experience. For now, though, let's look at communications media. As I suggested above, all communications media create a kind of subjectivity appropriate to them, be that subject or individual a listener, a reader, a viewer, or what have you. And of course listeners, readers, and viewers might eventually become speakers or singers, writers, or filmmakers, to pick only these examples. Communications media can and sometimes do work both ways. Senders can become receivers and vice versa.

Since communications media create subjectivities they also create communities, groups of people who interact via the medium, whatever it may be. As creators of community, communications media regulate a specific kind of self-social bond, they determine the nature and pace of self-social interaction, they delimit what can be said, when, by whom, and how. Beyond this, but as an extension of it, communications media also imply pedagogies, methods that not only train subjects to interact via the media but also essentially create those subjects by shaping their biological propensities, by providing literal channels through which we can express our desires.

Celebrity culture, of course, turns on this axis, on the fantasy of role reversal, the notion that one day I too might be more than a mere receiver, that I might be empowered to speak. This fantasy has only become more acute with the recent rise of reality shows. But the power of speech is closely guarded, a function of class, economics, ideology, and, most of all, connection. Enculturation ensures that those entrusted with the power of speech won't let the cat out of the bag, won't burst the ideological bubble or inadvertently deflate the discursive balloon.

None of these notions should sound particularly shocking. They have been floating around for a long time. Eric Havelock's brilliant 1963 book, *Preface to Plato*, explored them in the context of the transition from *mythos* to *logos*, from orality to literacy, in the classical Greek *paideuma* (Leo Frobenius' word for the complex vortex of notions that animate the morphology of a civilization). And Marshall McLuhan extended them across a career. His *Gutenberg Galaxy* (1962) charted the emergence of the modern "typographic" individual, while *Understanding Media* (1964) and *The Medium is the Massage* (1967), perhaps most famously, followed the breakdown of that form of subjectivity through the rise of what McLuhan loosely termed the "media," by which he generally meant a group of electronic technologies, including primarily television and radio. We should remember though that McLuhan also used the word "media" in a far more expansive sense, in a sense similar to what we mean by design, to reference any "extension" of human experience. In this sense, media studies should be capacious enough to offer attention to every element of the designed world. More generally however, and in common parlance, "media" means communications media and that limitation distinguishes media from design.

I say that none of these assumptions should sound particularly shocking and I bet that some of you are saying, not only aren't they shocking, they're banal. But others of you are skeptical, unwilling to grant so large a role in character formation to communications media or, I suspect, anything else. Some of this skepticism arises from the emptiness of the word "media" which has lost a great deal of its meaning in our "media saturated" world. Another bit of it arises from the condition that I am trying to diagnose, and hopefully clarify: the hegemony of design in contemporary culture. Media saturated we may be, but design nevertheless creates the context of our everyday lives. What's the difference? Media disseminates content, of a kind, while design creates form. The form of the media may determine the nature of the content, as McLuhan claimed, and hence also the nature of the receiving-sending subject and of the ensuing self-social bond, but design serves a more fundamental function in culture today: it creates the context in which the media may function. The media are in fact essentially a function of design, which does much more besides.

McLuhan's "typographic man," the subject who lives in the Gutenberg Galaxy, is the autonomous individual subject theorized during the European Enlightenment, the hegemonic communications media of which was of course the printing press: a machine used for making Bibles, novels, and newspapers, most significantly. The typographic man (following McLuhan's usage) is the self-reflective subject possessed of and created by his critical self-consciousness, itself a function of the imagination. The typographic man reads narratives and consumes images that are themselves representative microcosms of his own critical self-consciousness: whirlpools of self-reflection isolated from the totality of the world. Reading texts and images takes time, but this is ok, beneficial even. The typographic man is a rational and linear thinker, living in a period of history conceived in terms of linear progress. He is a mechanized man for a mechanized, industrialized time. He understands how representations work, at least in general, and thus has faith in representative politics and in conspicuous consumption, which is a correlate of the same basic structure. As Marx demonstrated, exchange functions metaphorically: this *equals* that in a world where all things can be understood as representations. "My objects, my self" is the mantra of the typographic man, who lives in a world of ordered signs of himself. Don Quixote *is* the library of chivalric romances he sealed off in his house. Mr. Darcy *is* Pemberley. Flaubert, as he said, *is* Madame Bovary.

McLuhan anticipated the collapse of this system. He anticipated the hegemony of a new communications media – *the* media – and a new form of subjectivity to go with it. Typographic man prioritized the eye over the ear, vision over hearing. His environment was directed rather than immersive. His attention intensive rather than extensive, delayed rather than instantaneous, individual and autonomous rather than tribal, local rather than global. McLuhan's new model of subjectivity would of course reverse all of these priorities.

This is all very interesting but it's still pretty easy to dismiss McLuhan, particularly if you actually read him. He too often buried brilliant aphorisms in meandering prose, or used examples that didn't always measure up to his insights. He became perhaps too popular for his own good at some point, a sound bite, a pundit who lost his punch. More importantly, for my argument, the culture shifted out from under him even as he was pointing to essential changes within it. He was a prophet of media in a time when television had three channels, radio was still predominantly AM, personal computers were more than a decade away, and personal audio devices like the SONY Walkman more than two decades away. None of this invalidates his fundamental insight – that technology makes the man – but it should temper our enthusiasm for it. A revolution in communications media has occurred since McLuhan's death in 1980 and even that revolution pales in comparison to the revolution in design of which it has been a part.

Looking back, we can see how we got here; we can trace our cultural steps, in terms of communications media, from Gutenberg to Google, though it might be more helpful if we started the story a little earlier in time. A very brief history of communications media might begin with the symbolic forms created by Paleolithic peoples, neatly divided as they were between the movable and the immoveable. (This is where Philip Meggs began his influential history of graphic design.) Portable forms included everything from small symbolic statuettes and carvings to clothing and body art and ornamentation. Non-moveable forms included parietal images, within caves and without. Surprisingly, the Paleolithic media offer some of the best analogies for understanding our world of design today. Though Paleolithic images may often be representational, the representations do not rely on narrative and their effects are situated within and intended for a specific total environment, whether it be a cave or a context more representative of everyday life. As with design today, the images serve to mark individual identities within the social group or to provoke a specific experience in a specific space. These are images designed for *interaction* rather than contemplation.

Communal spaces were at the center of the next revolution in communications media, that being the rise of symbolic architecture, whether funerary or religious. Tombs and temples were constructed to tell us something about ourselves and to stand the test of time, which they did. Writing was also a relatively early invention of the urban revolution, though the transition from orality to literacy did not occur, in the West, until the classical age in ancient Greece. Literacy did not however threaten to become anything akin to prominent until the end of the Middle Ages, when the printing press made books more common and thus less symbolic in and of themselves.

Across these latter periods, the codex form succeeded in part because it could be carried. Gutenberg and the graphic designers that followed his 1439 invention only intensified the effects of that fundamental form. Newspapers and novels appeared more or less simultaneously in the early seventeenth century as vehicles of information produced by moveable type. Oil paintings emerged as the functional image-based analog to these printed texts. Unlike woodcuts or engravings, oil paintings possess a richness and depth of color that satisfies the contemplative eye. They can be moved, and therefore sold. The Fine Art tradition shared a parallel history with the novel and newspapers as a companion of contemplative typographic man, who could carry his communications media with him.

The media as McLuhan knew it only began to emerge in the middle of the nineteenth century with the commercialization of the telegraph and the perfection and popularization of photography in the 1830s. Telephones and phonographs followed in the 1870s and motion pictures in the 1890s, by which time city streets where emblazoned with large, multi-color posters promoting all manner of products and entertainments. Industrially produced goods needed all the help they could get in differentiating themselves from their competitors, and the advertising industry was born to provide that help. By the 1890s, the then newly founded advertising agencies began to establish their own design departments. Radio and television were late comers to the scene. Commercial radio did not begin to spread until the early 1920s, and television not until the late 1930s and 1940s, in Europe and America. When McLuhan published *Understanding Media* in 1964, network television had been broadcasting for less than two decades in America. It was still a cool new topic.

Communications technologies in this era of mass media were technologies targeting masses of people: newspapers, film, and radio, each in their way, served to create communal experiences for nations as a whole. And I use the word "targeting" intentionally. McLuhan's media sent its messages down a one-way street. There was no way to talk back, no real way to participate without becoming part of the machine. Today's communications technologies on the other hand emphasize our participation, within certain limits, while simultaneously isolating us from others, and they do these things in many different ways. Mobile phones, iPods, and portable computers plugged into a wireless internet are ubiquitous and private. Television, whether satellite, cable, or online, can be tailored to personal preference with TiVo, and now offers such a plethora of choices that we can no longer count on the community implied by watching one of the same three channels our neighbors are watching. The VCR was essentially unknown to McLuhan but it already represents an archaic stepping-stone to this era for us.

When did our era of individualized-interactive communications media begin? Can we blame the Kodak Instamatic, first marketed in 1963, the camera that made photography so easy and affordable? Single lens reflex cameras began to democratize a more serious kind of amateur image-making later in the decade. Video games, personal computers and mobile phones were all developed from the mid-1970s to mid-1980s, the decade in which cable television began to spread and SONY introduced its first Walkman. In 1984, Apple debuted its MacIntosh, the first personal computer to use a visual interface and a mouse for navigation rather than a text-based command line. During these same years Adobe Systems developed software capable of describing all the elements on a page – lines, texts, images – in a homogenous way that made home desktop publishing a reality and that ultimately transformed the professional practice of graphic design. A decade later, Netscape Navigator made interconnectivity via the internet a viable and indeed exciting reality and smart phones let mobile users send email and browse the web on hand-held devices.

Our world has become still more interactive in the decade since then with, among other things, the introduction and popularization of TiVo, the spread of massively multiplayer online role-playing games (MMORPGs), and the new generation of interactive video game systems, lead by Nintendo's Wii. Of MMORPGs, World of Warcraft, which was released in its most familiar form in 2004, reports 11.5 million monthly subscribers worldwide. While this is a lot, it represents only 62% of the 18.5 million-member market for MMORPGs. These figures are of course *monthly*. Nintendo, for its part, sold 13.4 million of its Wii game consoles in the United States alone between November 2006 and November 2008. Wii is at present the bestselling interactive home video game system. Its motion sensitive controllers let multiple players physically interact by miming game motions. According to their own promotional figures, Nintendo has shipped 77 million Wii consoles to date. By contrast, note that 459,972 people visited the Metropolitan Museum of Art in New York between October 18 and December 31, 2005 to see *Vincent van Gogh: The Drawings*, a show that everyone involved would agree was outstandingly successful. When I suggest that we redirect our analytic attention to the material facts of the way that we live, these are the kinds of facts that I am talking about.

A colleague of mine from a history department put all of this in relief when he recently remarked, "our students don't even watch television anymore." Neither he nor I was particularly concerned about it. We don't really watch television either. In context, the substance of his remark was the observation that no center holds in our classrooms. No cultural references can be relied upon to bridge, as analogies, known and unknown spheres of knowledge. Nor can we count on cultural references to function as reliable paralogies, or models of distinction. Comparison and distinction, the warp and woof of education, have ceased to serve. They have ceased to serve because no cohesive communities of either speakers or listeners exist.

Academics today often cannot even agree on the right questions to ask one another about their respective fields. We frequently don't know enough about different disciplinary methods and concerns to enter into dialogue about them. Professional courtesy and, I think, a sense of bashful uncertainty keeps us from asking too many questions. Each of us has our own specialization, our own little ivy covered ivory silo, and we're content to assume that everyone else does too. This kind of polite, hands-off approach obviously isn't particularly helpful. And it is unlikely that television, the internet, or any other kind of media, will lead us – all of us – back to some promised land of communicative clarity. Design studies might however offer a more productive way to parse distinctions between disciplines and to help us begin to reorganize the academy.

My colleague's cultural baseline – television – is itself instructive. Were he perhaps a little older he might have mentioned the novel, lamenting the absence of the generally educated reader. Were he of a different mind, he might have mentioned popular music, pushing the oddly persistent notion that popular music has replaced poetry in culture since the 1960s. In fact, none of these communications media hold hegemonic sway over students or anyone else today. *Billboard* and *Publishers Weekly* might use the word bestseller, each in their way, but the word has nothing to do with cultural impact. MMORPGs and Wii divert us even more thoroughly than Harry Potter did.

As noted above, Marshall McLuhan often referred to media as *extensions* of man, in the sense of prosthetics. This metaphor is not quite right, neither for the mass media of the late modern age nor for the participatory media of our own. The mass media were extensions of the culture industry rather than extensions of individuals. They extended the power of previously empowered speakers rather than transforming disempowered listeners into speakers. And in our era of participatory media, the media are not extensions of subjectivity but rather dissimulators of it. Our faith in subjectivity is always misplaced. The media are channels that conduct our energies without creating or maintaining our subjectivity beyond the thin veil of a digital avatar.

Communications media, in short, create forms of subjectivity, subjects and communities. They do this by providing a field of self-reflection, a means of self-recognition via representation, a stable space in which one may say "I am that," whether that be a Homeric hero, a Spanish hidalgo, or some other icon of identity, be it Brando or Bardot. These media have evolved in our time from forms of representation, operating on a mass scale a century ago, to forms of participation in a special sense of this term. Participatory or interactive media structure our engagements with them without necessarily structuring the subjectivity that is engaged. We don't after all mistake ourselves for our Wii avatar nor do we stare contemplatively into the screen of our iPod as we watch videos there. In this sense, participatory media is a more accurate phrase than interactive media. We participate in the sense that we actually make choices but this is not really interactivity: the machines don't change and we don't really either.

Significantly, this transition has taken place while our cultural institutions – our schools, libraries, and museums in particular – have remained focused on and organized around older forms of representational media and, lately, fixated on expanding or "diversifying" the range of representations represented. Such gestures are symptomatic of our continued fetishism of representational cultural forms and of our unwillingness to change the basic structure and orientation of our thought. Along these lines, McLuhan claimed that new media always begin by translating the content of the old media into a new form. Early writing repeated oral tales. Films quickly learned to repeat the narrative structures and strategies of novels. This kind of replacement haunts our own era as well. A couple of years ago, Jeffery Katzenberg proclaimed 3-D technology as the future of film, manifesting a wish to save the theatrical release of his cherished cultural form from the threat of new technologies of image distribution. An article in the *New York Times* (10-6-08) compared playing video games, like MMORPGs, to reading, though the two activities are manifestly not analogous. This comparison also animates attempts to discuss video games as new forms of narrative art. Another form of this same phenomenon is found in the common notion of convergence. Convergence implies

the homogenization of media content across diverse distribution platforms even though those platforms inevitably change
the content. These are all instances of the fetishism of cultural
forms, some longstanding, others relatively new, examples of
an inability to think without blinders on, to approach new cultural forms directly. In each case, the point is to put the genii
back in the bottle.

I'm suggesting that we try to redirect our fetishism of cultural forms, most notably our fetishism of forms of representation: paintings, sculptures, novels, poems, plays, and the like.
My point is not to say that these forms are no longer pleasurable
either as historical artifacts or contemporary expressions, but
rather to suggest that the longstanding cultural cache granted
them might be tempered by the reflection that none of these
forms continues to serve the social function that it once did. No
matter how much we may enjoy these forms, they no longer occupy the same cultural space or serve the same cultural purpose.
Our continued fascination with these media – and here I really
am talking about the energy exerted by our college curricula
rather than by any genuine cultural fascination – serves only as
a distraction from the truly significant elements of our world.

The base media of our world have changed from mass media
to interactive media and these new forms of media have emerged
within a total context determined by design. The paintings, poems, novels and newspapers valued by typographic man reflect
historical conditions that have not been ours for since at least
the end of World War Two, if not in fact much earlier. As I have
already observed, these forms were invented in the *early* modern
era, the *seventeenth* century. The novel arguably reached its peak
as a cultural form as long ago as 1813, with *Pride and Prejudice*, or
perhaps in 1881, with *The Brothers Karamazov*. It has been even
longer since poetry was widely celebrated as the central bearer

of cultural codes. This is not a question of taste. It is a question of cultural currency, of coin of the realm.

The solitary early modern citizen was replaced by the shocked and alienated late modern *masses* in the early twentieth century. In the second half of the twentieth century, the masses themselves were replaced by an entirely new form of subjectivity, the subjectivity created by and at work in an interactive culture of design. From contemplation to mediation to interaction, this is the motion of our culture over the last four hundred years: from the contemplation of representations to an immersion in design.

Interactive media and design are not representational forms. Graphic design may occasionally use representations but these representations are imbedded within a total context that is the essential product of design. Paintings, photographs, and poetry, in other words, fall under the aegis of design, rather than the other way around. Design determines the total horizon of our experience. It structures the space and the pace of our lives. Design shapes the disposition of our energies like a vortex, in Ezra Pound's sense of this term: a point of maximum energy shaped by multiple and intersecting material and ideological forces of input, constriction, and output.

My purpose is not to offer design up as a new idol but rather to point to it as an open and evolving nexus of common concern. This distinction is important. Many of the writers associated with design today decidedly do hold their field of interest up as an idol. To do so, they must isolate it from other forms of cultural activity, generally through an appeal to the existing social discourses about design, which is to say the discourses of functionalism (industrial design) and communicative clarity (graphic design) and so on. These discourses, needless to say, aren't as useful as they are intended to be in understanding design objects, which cannot be fully understood in purely utilitarian terms. Design objects are always more than what they do.

But more importantly, the effort to isolate design objects involves transforming those objects into representations, treating industrial design like sculpture, graphic design like painting or literature, interactive websites, including video games, again like painting or literature. The recent academic fascination with video games is among the most obvious cases of the kind of inappropriate fetishism that I'm talking about. Video games seem to possess elements familiar to other forms – the visual content of painting, the pseudo-narrative content of literature – yet they are created and function in a completely different ways. By focusing on the apparently familiar world of video games we lose sight of the fact that video games are in fact so unfamiliar and that they are far closer to the world of design – they are part of it – than they are to either Fine Art or literature. By focusing on video games we also fail to see all of the other interesting things that are happening on the internet, all of the other sites and spaces that entice, challenge and inform us in new ways. In order to turn our thoughts to design, we need to let go of the familiar models of inquiry and the familiar models of idolatry that characterized our approach to Fine Art: we need to begin to think beyond representation.

The design disciplines establish the total context for human life in our time. Lest we retain a fantasy of some frontier wilderness, let's remember that design decisions regulate our interaction with and preservation of the wild. If the wilderness is to be preserved, as it must be, it will be preserved by design. The word design in the sense I'm using it does not describe a single phenomenon, a singular mode of cultural activity, but rather a diversity of related phenomena and cultural activities, pursued, promoted, and understood in myriad ways. If culture is a complex of behaviors and material objects, design can be understood as the activity that creates the context for those behaviors and that creates those objects. Design, in this sense, creates culture, as frivolous or fulsome as this might be. There is no place, no thought that is beyond the world of design.

Design Culture

Design decisions shape every aspect of the way that we live. For better or worse, all of the things around us were created by design, which is to say both intentionally and by actual people. Tables and chairs, computers, clothes and cars, you name it, someone – generally a group of people – invested time and energy, maybe a little, maybe a lot, in making it. Even our encounters with nature are structured by design decisions made by gardeners, landscapers, park planners, the park service, and the urban planners who built the highway we took to get to the wilderness. Bill McKibben called this the end of nature, but it is really the beginning of design.

Not everyone who makes design decisions recognizes him or herself as a designer nor do we always recognize these individuals – or ourselves in these roles – as designers. Sometimes design decisions occur in isolation, but more often they are made by several designers of different kinds working together or, even more likely, in series, making decisions in response to other decisions. All of this is to say that we live in a designed culture and we aren't really aware of the ways in which and the extent to which design shapes our lives.

To put the matter simply, design decisions give form to the way we live. They create the material context in which we exercise our judgment and our passions. They give material shape to our thoughts, feelings, and sensations, which is to say that they create culture, the complex aggregate of our thoughts and actions.

This obvious fact is something we deny or ignore at our peril. Design decisions are choices made by designers. But designers work for clients, some good, some bad, some corporate, some governmental, some for profit, some not-for-profit: clients, in short, across the social spectrum. Where there is room for choice, there is room for error, and for all its marvels, design culture is a room full of errors, some worse than others.

And yet, as John Thackara put it on the first page of his book, *In the Bubble: Designing in a Complex World*, "If we can design our way into difficulty, we can design our way out." Thackara is primarily talking about industrial design and systems engineering, about the way that we collectively use our resources and about the alarming rate at which we are polluting our environment and using our resources up. It is undoubtedly more productive to hope Thackara's faith in our abilities is justified than to fear the opposite. Design might be part of the problem, but it is also part of the solution: it might even be all of it.

Design might be *all* of the solution because design functions in concert with human desire. Design is only part of the problem because human desire is the other part. But design might be all of the solution because design can shape desire. Design activates human desire, harnesses it, channels it, and may ultimately even have the power to transform it, within the limits of human biology. This should not strike us as a horrifying thought. *Design culture is a culture of give and take in which no one – not designers, their clients, or the members of the community of consumers – has absolute power.* Another way to say this is to say that design always expresses itself against resistances and never by leaps and bounds, rather by micro-steps, expressions of fragile and unstable micro-freedoms, ever ripe for repetition, reinforcement, or reversal.

Economist Richard Thaler and legal scholar Cass Sunstein have demonstrated the power of design to affect desire in their book *Nudge*. A "nudge" is a design solution to an aspect of human behavior that is unlikely to shift without the nudge. Images of flies were etched into the urinals in the men's room at the Amsterdam airport, for example, right near the drains, to offer users a target of sorts and thereby to discourage "spillage." Unsurprisingly, the solution worked and spillage dropped by 80%. The nudge, in this case the painted flies, shifted human behavior by exploiting human desire and channeling it down a more "productive" path. Significantly, nudges don't involve education or training, they don't offer or require incentives, and they don't make you do anything that you don't want to do already. Nudges aren't ideas that require the support of complex arguments nor are they didactic in any way. Nudges don't nudge you by changing your ideas about the world, they don't persuade, convince or cudgel. Nor do nudges exploit an if-then theatrical scenario: nudges don't ask you to perform a role. Nothing is fake. The nudge simply offers you a chance to do what you want to do anyway. A nudge does however exploit that desire toward the best possible end, within a limited situation. The nudge is a good example of the way that design culture works in general.

With this kind of thing in mind, I'd like to make a few general observations about the culture of design.

> Design culture is simultaneously both material and ideological: it is inherently heterogeneous.

> Design culture is not singular, unified, or totalizing.

> Design culture is nodal, networked, and open, rather than hegemonic, hierarchical, and closed.

> Design culture is never fully present nor ever absent.

> Design culture is not representational, though it may include representations.

> Design culture requires personal and communal participation.
>
> Design culture does not exploit, create, or imply a critically reflective autonomous individual.
>
> Design culture is fluid and inherently unstable.

I think it might be helpful to work our way through this list, in particular because so many of these notions fly in the face of the way that many if not in fact most design writers and cultural critics write about design. Rather than structure this description around praise for or criticisms of specific writings by design writers, I also think it might be more helpful and expeditious to address each point in turn in a purely positive manner.

Design culture is simultaneously both material and ideological.

Design decisions give shape to ideas. Generally these ideas originate with a client of one kind or another. Even if the designer originates the idea him or herself, the client function remains distinct from that of the designer, who creates the material embodiment of the idea for a manufacturer to manufacture. Design is ideological in the loose sense that it is the embodiment of ideas and also in the more technical sense of the term, that it embodies ideas that are themselves part of an overarching, non-scientific social ideology. Progressive or Leftist oppositional writing about design often blames the messenger, faulting designers for the ideologies of their clients, and reciprocally forgetting that designers are part of the process without being all of the process. But the origination of the idea is less significant to me than the fact that design objects lend material form to thoughts. If we are interested in design, we should probably focus our interest on the material forms involved rather than on the ideas they purport to convey.

Along these lines, for example, graphic design is typically celebrated as a vehicle of clear and compelling communication, placing the emphasis on the final word in the phrase, communication. Yet, as material embodiments of a message, graphic design objects are sensuous material first and abstract communicative signs second. The texture of the material often speaks first and most loudly. We are seduced by the look and feel of a book before we read the first word. We are guided in our response to the work by the way that it looks, by the material of which it is made. All of these material aspects of the work shape the total context in which the ideas contained in the work circulate. Dag Söderberg's recent *Bible Illuminated*, for the Swedish publisher Forlaget Illuminated, for example, presents the text of the New Testament in the form of a fashion or lifestyle magazine. Similarly, a few years ago, the Poetry Foundation in Chicago attempted to lure a wide variety of popular magazines to start publishing poetry in their pages as many of them once did, with splashy spreads. In each case, the popular graphic style contrasts with the content of the works, to positive or negative effect depending on one's perspective.

More abstractly, the science of aesthetics, which is to say the science of sensations, teaches us that images affect us emotionally, and hence also intellectually, in purely visual, thus material or physical, ways. El Lissitzky's abstract and geometric Prouns, for example, were intended to convey ideas through the dynamic interplay of colored geometric shapes. Visual language like this can speak without words, through volume, line, and color, through presence and absence. Artists, art critics and historians have been studying these effects in the Fine Arts for centuries, yet the language of aesthetic criticism has yet to fully penetrate the self-understanding of graphic design as a field due to the ideology of communicative clarity to which that field is beholden.

Graphic designers are trained to claim that they are communicators first and foremost even though they are in fact motivators first and foremost. They make ideas compelling with purely formal means and this is the basis of their craft. A graphic designer activates desire visually well before communicating clear and distinct ideas. More forcefully put, the graphic designer inserts a compelling *resistance to communication* into a communicative object. The resistance makes the imaginative mind leap into and become involved with the work. All this in mind, graphic design is first and foremost a language of forms rather than a means of simple and direct communication.

A similar argument can be made in regard to the utilitarian ideology of functionalism in other design disciplines, from industrial design to architecture. As material embodiments of ideas, these forms, whether they be houses or house-wares, are things first and thoughts second. The allure of an object often has less to do with its function than with the ways that it feels in our hand or the ways that it engages with our self-contradictory desires, like the uniquely balanced need we each have to find shelter in a space that is enclosed without being enclosing.

Design, in short, often has less to do with function than it does with the look and feel of a thing. A few years ago, Robert Lutz said as much, when he took over as CEO of General Motors: "I see us being in the art business," he said, "Art, entertainment and mobile sculpture, which, coincidentally, also happens to provide transportation" (quoted in Danny Hakim, "An Artiste Invades Stodgy G.M." *New York Times* 10.19.01). One hundred years ago, as we have seen, Marinetti claimed that a racing car was more beautiful than the Victory of Samothrace. His words stretched out across a new horizon of human experience, into a new design culture, a culture that we now inhabit.

Because design culture is simultaneously material and ideological it activates our desire on several levels simultaneously. It speaks to us physically, through form and texture, and it speaks to us intellectually, by activating cultural associations derivative of formal elements and by evoking a trajectory of engagement, of use. While it makes sense to begin a discussion of design with the basic material facts about the object in question, the other elements cannot be ignored. To prioritize any one of these elements at the expense of the others is to misapprehend the nature of the designed object and thus also of design. But design writers frequently do just that. A more holistic approach to design would endeavor to describe design objects as embodiments of the contradictions that animate them: material/ideological, physical/abstract, object/sign. Graphic design is often most exciting when its forms challenge its message. Industrial design objects are often most compelling when they seem to challenge their own functional utility. This is the inherent heterogeneity of the designed object.

Additionally, and as I've already said, designed objects are heterogeneous in point of origin and in ultimate value: they are the products of the combined and often compromised talents of clients and designers working in concert and they are creations that benefit from so many types of appeal, physical, intellectual, and emotional, that one cannot summarize their meaning succinctly.

Design culture is not singular, unified, or totalizing.

With all of these diverse forces active in the creation and appreciation of a designed object, one cannot convincingly claim that design culture is singular, unified, or totalizing in its powers or even intent. There are simply too many people with too many diverse interests at work as producers and consumers for this to be the case. Perhaps the thought of totality itself is a paranoid fantasy. I'm not saying that we should banish the thought of totality from our minds, only that we need to temper it, add nuance to it, through a genuine awareness of the processes of design. To do so is to recognize the micro-freedoms inherent in the design process, the push-back that the designer can effect against a client's wishes, and the creativity that the designer can bring to the process.

In *No Logo*, Naomi Klein demonstrated the broad reach of multi-national corporations in determining the specific qualities of contemporary design culture. Her book begins with the insight that, over the past twenty or so years, the most successful corporations have gradually stopped making things and started cultivating their brands. A brand is the "core idea" of a corporation, the notion at the center of a corporate identity. Nike, famously, aspires to stand in for "fitness" rather than "shoes." It is more profitable for a company like Nike to label goods produced in some far off corner of the globe than to produce and label those goods in the United States. What matters most is consumer identification with the brand. As manufacturing costs go down, advertising costs go up, and the products themselves tend toward a kind of disembodiment. As brand-value increases, actual product value decreases. A process of dematerialization subsumes the things of the world. This is true and worrisome. But it must be remembered that design culture is material culture, and that the objects and advertisements that bear brands will never be completely dematerialized, they can't be. To the extent that people become aware of design they are becoming aware of and attentive to the physical nature of things. The design process itself stands in the way of branded dematerialization. I'll come back to this notion once we have a fuller sense how design culture works.

My point for the moment is simply that design culture is grounded in a physical reality that cannot be completely subsumed by corporate culture. Our struggle against the supposed hegemony of multi-national corporations is ultimately less an ideological struggle than a material one. Again, the mistake of many Left oppositional writers derives from a lack of design awareness. The ultimate weapon, on both sides of this struggle, is the education of design awareness, the education of sensibility, the cultivation of taste. Design education is an education in the things of the world and the processes that produce them. Awareness of these things and processes produces attentiveness to them.

Design culture is nodal, networked, and open, rather than hegemonic, hierarchical, and closed.

Design objects function as physical points of connectivity in a networked culture that must be understood as a libidinal economy, an economy of desire. Unlike paintings, for example, design objects do not aspire to isolate themselves from the world. Rather, they aspire to integrate themselves into it at specific points.

Designed objects are designed to call attention to themselves, that is to attract and activate desire. They call out to and lure consumers but that call is not the call of a carnival barker inviting customers into a closed tent. It is the call of the conductor inviting everyone aboard while signaling the location of a switch. Design objects thus function as relays or channels through which desire flows. Ezra Pound's notion of a vortex is apposite. A vortex is an organization or disposition of energy in space, composed of many disparate and diverse material and ideological forces. It does not "cohere" in any logical sense. But it serves to lure and focus cultural forces, the energies of production and consumption, for good or ill. R. Buckminster Fuller used the word "knot" in a similar fashion. A knot is an organization of energy folded and looped back into and around itself, a disposition of force organized in such a way as to regulate the flow of that force, to accelerate or decelerate its transformation. Both of these models are distinctly open, they attract and accept forces or energies, resources, materials, thoughts, from various and diverse spheres. They gather these forces into a point of intersection that is greater than the sum of its parts and disperse them outward from there along trajectories that may resemble those that fed the forces into the system but that more than likely will not. Producers and consumers, in other words, share a point of intersection – a designed object – but that may be all.

As points of intersection, designed objects aspire to distinction and uniqueness, but this is a separation that does not require isolation. Here again we are talking about the paradox of design: the fact that designed objects are strictly speaking never what they are, never fully distinct from culture, never fully integrated into it. To the extent that a designed object is fully integrated into a cultural space it will be unnoticed, taken for granted, it will fail to attract attention and to function at the highest level of its capacities. It will become inert as an active force and as an activator of force. Our eyes, for example, grow tired of reading the same typefaces day after day; so graphic designers use different typefaces to pique our curiosity and lure us into texts. The very strangeness of the letterforms holds our interest, at least for a while.

Here again, the physical diversity of design culture is derivative of its function and essentially heterogeneous. Along these lines, design culture cannot aspire to *closure*, to achieving a complete or final solution to any problem in design, for the necessity of change is built into the system as a law of dynamics. Even the most utopian of designers – one thinks of Le Corbusier's "city of tomorrow" or Jan Tschichold's "new typography" – modified their views across the length of their careers as they shifted the focus of their interest from one pole of the design equation to the other, from material concerns to ideological ones, from the allure of rationalism to the appeal of chance, from logical necessity to cultural tradition, as base motives and limits to design. But design is paradox or it is nothing and our thinking about design must embrace the challenge of this paradox or we will misunderstand it.

Design culture is never fully present nor ever absent.

We have noted the ubiquity of design. A world without logos is not an option nor is it a good idea. More realistically, we need to know how to support the right brands, the brands with the best design.

The notion that design culture is never fully present is more complex. Nodal, networked design culture is always pointing beyond itself. Design objects attract our desire for them but also and more often they attract our desire for something else, not some other object like them but some other thing or activity entirely. We like a certain car because of the technological and cultural associations it conjures, but we also like it for what it lets us do. We like a chair because it implies and attracts a relationship with our body in space as well as from the technological and cultural associations it conjures. We like a poster not only for the way that it looks, but for what it looks toward, for the thing that it signals, that for which it is only a sign.

The relays of design culture are interchanges that function on the model of dissemination. They are always at once present and absent. They are powerful in themselves but dependent upon something that is absent, that is only suggested by them. Even something as banal as a government document derives its power in part from its physical nature and in part from the network of cultural information and activity in which it circulates. Present and absent at once, design objects derive their meaning from a split context, the immediate material location in which they can be found and the broader social and temporal continuum with which they form a broken continuity. They are at once viscerally here and vigorously pointing beyond themselves.

This is one reason why design objects resist archival presentation. To place a design object in a museum is to deny it access to both of the contexts from which it derives its meaning. The white box was itself designed to support the isolation that is the essence of Fine Art experience. The Fine Art object intends to separate itself from the bustle of everyday life and the hushed corridors of galleries and museums aid and abet it in this enterprise. Design objects on the other hand seek connection and interconnection and they actually depend upon it. Doubly deprived of context, of lived situation and of the social sphere, design objects often fall flat as pseudo-sculptures or pseudo-paintings. Gathering a number of them together, creating a kind of room within a room within a museum, accentuates the problem without resolving it. We still don't know how to look at them.

Ironically, this is also why the most exciting museums today are exciting for their architecture or for the design related activities that they house. In design culture, we are more accustomed to being moved by design than by the contemplation of static works. The building works on us more than the works do. Similarly, children's museums are so much fun for this reason. Children's museums aren't museums at all. They are design work-shops, temples to interaction and involvement: activities include drawing or illustration, modeling objects in clay, experiments in spatial relationships, mazes, interactive light shows and mirrors all of which invite our minds and bodies to participate.

The art historical enterprise, from which design history has derived its methods and mandate, is fundamentally at odds with the nature of design. Art historians are fetishists of artifacts but a design object will only function as a fetish if it has been deprived of its place in living culture. A fetish stands in place of something absent, it creates culture where none exists. A design object on the other hand signals its own absence, its own status as dependent upon something else, something beyond itself, whether an activity or an object.

I make these remarks without the slightest tinge of nostalgia. We live in a new kind of culture and we might as well get used to it. The excitement of this culture is born on wings of design and bored if deprived of a means to participate in it.

Design culture is not representational, though it may include representations.

Graphic design incorporates images and texts and in this enterprise it has access to the entire range of possible images: drawn or painted illustrations, photographs, scientific images, all of greater or lesser complexity or quality. By integrating images and texts into a combined object, graphic design does not function as a representational form of making, though it uses representations to achieve its effects. The other design arts too use representations of various kinds in various ways. Robert Venturi and Denise Scott Brown have argued for an iconographic architecture, for understanding and creating architecture as a sign system. One might situate their work historically at a post-modern turn in cultural history, a moment when things tended toward the ideological or informational pole of the design equation. But they also argue for a complexity in architecture derived from the heterogeneity of materials and methods. Their sign systems are multiple and interactive, and hence unstable. The logic of representation on the other hand is a logic of stability. Representations, of whatever kind, capture and fix in an image or analogy something that inherently resists capture. The poet Arthur Rimbaud famously sought to "fix frenzies in their flight," an agenda that provides a pointed contrast to that of the design fields. Design seeks to activate energies rather than to congeal them for contemplation. Even when design objects invite us to think about what we are doing with them this thought is secondary to the action. Here I am thinking of graphic design objects that are so reticent to communication that one must ponder them intently to be rewarded with information, as in David Carson's more indulgent pieces. Even within the design specialization of information design, design objects do not function on the model of representation. Information architectures do not aspire to stand in for the world, rather they navigate through a portion of it. The excitement of information design is in cutting this kind of clear path and, moreover, in creating an object – a chart, a graph or table – that activates a user within it.

*Design culture requires both personal and communal
participation.*

We activate design culture ourselves and we always have. There never was a mass-man, not in the way that we typically use the term. Mass production does not require mass consumption nor mass consumption mass production. The theory of reification is too simple. We have always dominated the products we purchase, always integrated them into a larger and more intricately chaotic life than their makers imagined, always used them for purposes beyond those for which they were intended. Michel de Certeau called this "poaching" and it has always been part of the life of things. In his Auschwitz memoir, *Se questo è un uomo* (If this is a man), Primo Levi movingly reminds his reader that the things we collect around ourselves, the trinkets and memorabilia, but also our clothes, our furniture, our objects, everything is part of the shell of our identity. We make things our own first through selection at the point of purchase, when we integrate those things into our complex, messy and overstuffed lives, and later with the wear and tear of use. It is interesting, I think, that very little of this has anything to do with the ideational content of a design object. We do not savor design for what it says to us but rather for what it does and for what it lets us do. A design object is an open opportunity for engagement and that is what we like about it.

Of course some design objects lend themselves to personalization better than others. Some designers conceive of this as a value and aspire to create objects that invite a greater degree of personalization than others. But not all objects were meant to bear with us over time, so we cannot hold this, or anything else really, up as a make or break principle of good design. The breaking point here is the point where the design object no longer serves to convey information from a client to a consumer, the point where the work simply invites consumer participation or consumption. At this point the work can only be described as a work of design in some very loose sense. Architect Rem Koolhaas offers a more positive example: he uses the word junkspace to describe architectural spaces that are so amorphous that they fail to create engagement and that are so rigid that they cannot be reinvented. Koolhaas himself obviously aspires to create architecture that is not junkspace. His architecture creates intense engagement and, at its best, permits some kind of evolutionary change at a future date. His Seattle Public Library, for example, was designed to facilitate the growth of the library's collections of books and other materials in a specific but non-rigid way.

The design object is a curious object in that it is the product of at least three distinct agencies: the client who motivates the work, the designer who designs it, and the consumer who activates it. The three agencies together function as a heterogeneous community, a mixed multitude. The designer functions as a bridge between the client and the consumer. The client has an idea that lacks material form, the designer creates that form, bringing the message or object to life in such a way that the consumer will recognize and receive it. The client inevitably has a specific target audience for the created object in mind, an ideal consumer. The designer knows not only how to create an object but also how to create an object that will reach the specific target audience. Designers create within the constraints of clients and consumers.

Earlier, I used the word "compromise" to describe the designer's task, but I did not intend it to be taken negatively. In order to convey an idea most appropriately a designer must find the design language that the target audience will recognize. This is not a question of personal taste nor does it entail the betrayal of personal taste. It is a matter of effective communication and in such matters the designer never enjoys absolute freedom. This is not a bad thing. Indeed, I find this to be one of the most interesting and exciting aspects of design culture. Designers bring people together. They bring consumers of a particular thing together as a group of users. But they also bring clients and consumers together in a special way. For a graphic designer, this may involve conveying a client message to a group of readers in the most powerful and effective way. For an architect it may mean creating an environment that will allow consumers to access a client's goods, whether this be in the context of a store, a museum or a public space. In each case, it is a question of community, or more precisely of integrating a personal message into a communal design discourse. This is the essence of design.

I say this is the essence of design and yet this is also one of the most derided aspects of design practice. As I noted earlier, in the context of a panel presentation at a recent conference, for example, a famous designer told several members of her audience that they were being "oppressed" by working for clients, suggesting that they should instead look deeply into themselves to discover who they are and then to express that. She had imported this fantasy of self-expression into design from the liberal democratic discourse of the Fine Art tradition without stopping to think about the actual social function of the designer. The ultimate irony of the moment, for me, was in the fact that both discourses were concerned with the problem of community, one representing the Enlightenment ideal of liberal democracy, the other the contemporary reality of the designer client community. These communities are of course distinct and in many ways incompatible with one another. But they are both communities nonetheless.

Yet the community that is created by and implicit in the success of the design process is a community that is not a community in the traditional sense. It is a post-Enlightenment form of community. It is not a question of being together in any physical way, for the designer the client and the consumer never meet. It is not a question of adhering to any set of beliefs, for again the three partners in this exchange need not share any specific values in common beyond their shared responsiveness to a certain kind of design. The communal force that is active within the designer client community is a force that links people together along a trajectory of conscious or unconscious engagement, the almost valueless value of appreciation and interest that drives culture at the most basic level.

The value that can be articulated with the phrase "I like that" is a value that is activated by design decisions and it is a value that cuts to the core of our identities as individuals without ever cohering into a larger, more solidified and recognizable system of values. Can we describe a group of individuals based on the cars they drive, the clothes they wear, or the foods they eat? Undoubtedly. Do these things compare with statements that individuals might make about "higher" things, like the nature of the god they believe in? Undoubtedly not. But significantly both types of value and valuation are co-present in culture, each active in its own way in different contexts. My point here is not to claim that we don't need to study the history of religious ideas but only that design decisions shape us in subtle and intricate ways and that we should devote more attention to them alongside our interest in the more recognized and for now recognizable areas of cultural studies.

Design culture does not exploit, create, or imply a critically reflective autonomous individual.

The modern world was a world of critically reflective autonomous individuals. Every aspect of modern culture from politics to poetics by way of the arts and sciences implied this one type of individual subjectivity. Even modern theology invented a "personal" god. The autonomy of the individual was reflected in the theory of the autonomous Fine Art object. But design objects are not autonomous objects. Nodal, networked and open, design objects imply a subjectivity that is as malleable as the objects themselves. Put somewhat bluntly, the subject of design is not one: by which I mean that the subject of design is not a singular, autonomous subjectivity. We all contain multitudes and those multitudes are activated by design. Clothes transform their wearers. Buildings move their occupants, actively or passively, physically or in revelry.

The lure of design is not reflection or recognition but rather the relay effected by the object, the transfer of energy and imagination, of subjective engagement, from presence to absence and back, always at work in design objects. The isolated images and narratives of the modern world helped create and support the autonomous individual. But the images and texts of graphic design don't operate in the same way. Rather, they interact in the consumer imagination and become active in referral.

Design culture is a culture of relays and referrals, of references and dissemination. Well designed spaces may present spectacular tableaux but they invite participation: the disruption and activation of those tableaux, the motion of a scene from one perspective to another, as in cinema, where a slightly shifted camera can alter the entirety of a shot.

Related to this, we can observe that celebrity culture is part of design culture not because it proposes an image in place of reality but because it suggests that one may live life for the deferred moment in which an image may appear and then later look back on the moment in which that image was captured, or more likely look forward again to some new image. The images were never intended to coincide with the self, they were never meant to be images with which one might identify. The deferral and eclipse of identity is often the precise point of the exercise. Similarly, much of the exhibitionism on the Internet is not about egotism but its precise opposite: the flight from the fragile self, wherein the phrase 'look what I did' is disconnected from 'look who I am'.

Design objects here fulfill our love of alterity, our longing to escape from the self, to plunge into the imagined experience of the not I. The sign of design is an invitation, a seduction, a lure beyond the self. Designers create great mirrors not because of the reflective surfaces but because of the shapes and presentation, the accompaniments that make the mirror so compelling to the viewer who wants to look not at the self but beyond it. Designed objects are experiences in abeyance, waiting to happen. This appeal is reified in the partial and fragmentary nature of design culture. Open and networked, design culture never closes, never coheres.

But this is not to say that the consumer of design lacks agency. On the contrary, the culture of consumption is driven by consumer demand. Alvin Toffler wanted to remind consumers of their power when he coined the word "prosumer." A prosumer is a consumer who votes with his or her dollars, who sees every trip to the market as an intervention into culture, an act of conscious and unconscious value-making. Design culture requires participation. It wants you. Without you nothing happens. So make the most of it. Do your part. To purchase a product is to insert yourself into an entire network of production and consumption. Living without is not an option. The only viable option is viable consumption. The writer William S. Burroughs often asked rhetorically, "Who am I to be critical? To live," he said, "is to collaborate." This statement is distinct from Johanna Drucker's notion of the ambiguous parallel complicity of the contemporary art world. For Burroughs, collaboration is participation. Burroughs saw his work as a search for points of intersection, where vectors of interest and energy converge and diverge in continual mutation. If collaboration is endemic to the system, the only enemy is stasis and mutation our only weapon against it. Consumption in this model is a "technology of the self," a way of experiencing and modifying one's identity and desires. This assertion does not advocate an orgy of absurd spending but rather an understanding of all activity as significant experience. Something as simple as shopping for shoes is a form of soul-making, an engagement with the world.

Design culture is fluid and inherently unstable.

Design culture came about, particularly in the decades following World War Two, as global capital attained a new degree of interconnectedness and fluidity. Rapid and intense developments in manufacturing, communications, and transportation technology launched this new world and now we are in it for good. This isn't to say that we are stuck with things as they are, with the economics and politics of the modern era, with its moribund educational and social institutions, its broken social infrastructure. Hardly. Broken or breaking, obsolete or inefficient, these structures are in a state of rapid transformation before our very eyes. Registering, tracking and even regulating these transformations exceeds our present concern, which is limited to the role of design culture in establishing the new economic, political, and social structures. The relationship between our awareness of design processes and political realities should be clear enough.

To promote awareness of design processes is to promote awareness of design culture. Design culture is, I think, best understood on the model of what Georges Bataille called "general economy." General economy measures whole systems, which is to say the interaction of many distinct and often apparently interconnected smaller, limited or restricted systems. Within such a framework one would track the "real cost" of an object as well as the total trajectory of that object, from resource to refuse, or ideally reuse. Awareness of design processes implies attention to every stage in the manufacture of goods or the implementation of services rather than attention narrowly focused on the apparent "bottom line". An appreciation of design implies an appreciation of design objects but also of the entire trajectory of object production, dissemination and reuse. And of course attention to these processes also implies an interest in our own role in these processes as designers, clients, or members of the community. The general economy of design culture is an economy of interconnectivity and interaction.

The nodes and networks of this cultural economy are constantly shifting with discovery, innovation, and consumer interest. The notion of a steady-state or stable design culture is slightly misleading given the constant and necessary vitality of these processes. Points of intersection – the nodes in the network – are points of transformation, wherein energy is transformed from one state to another. Depending on your location along the line or trajectory of development you might perceive these moments of transformation as incidents of exchange, expenditure or waste, but waste, in the memorable words of William McDonough and Michael Braungart, is food. Commercial exchange is never equal or innocent, labor cannot be transformed into goods purely and simply, the network is always open. And waste never really goes away, or at least it probably shouldn't. Waste is another form of wealth, waiting to be harnessed and activated by the culture of design.

The general economy of design culture is a libidinal economy, an economy driven by desire. The cultivation of design awareness and sensitivity is of course the cultivation of desire. The question we ultimately have to ask ourselves is what do we want? Recognizing and attending to the role of design in shaping our desires. The general economy of design culture is an economy of energies in constant transformation, forces colliding, commingling and contrasting with one another along trajectories of flight and fancy. Design objects are always located somewhere between two poles of the design equation: neither functional nor functionless, neither purely material nor purely motivated by ideas; neither purely personal nor purely communal, neither universal nor local, neither timeless nor ephemeral, neither insistently intense nor completely open. Design awareness is awareness of these contradictions. It might also entail an interest in exploring them, inserting our interest into the world of things that embody the extremes of each polarity, to each find our own needs and comforts therein.

Left oppositional writing often too quickly dismisses the positive role of design in culture, too quickly equates design with the processes of capitalism, to easily mistakes design with "designer", taking the word designer to signify a branded ensemble of stylistic tropes, in other words, an ideological formation. Brand managers, also, often harness design to disembody things, while the Left opposition dismisses design *tout court* as complicit with this process. But this is only a small portion of what design does in the world and is in fact contrary to the nature and function of design. Designers make things. The branding process will always fail to completely disembody branded things. The branding process tends toward the disembodiment of objects, the transformation of things into representations of ideas. Design awareness is an awareness of immanence, the material reality of things, held out as a temper against ideology.

Awareness of design entails an ability to perceive the total economy implied by an object, the "real cost" of the objects: the resources required to make it, the hand of the maker, the environmental processes of manufacturing, the necessities of distribution, the total communal impact of a specific point of sale. Awareness of design also entails an awareness of the material and ideological aspects of the object, a simultaneous awareness of both material texture and cultural meaning.

Design awareness is awareness of the human hand that shapes our lived world, at every step of the way, from resource to retail to reuse. The pleasure we take in design is, in large part, pleasure taken in our engagement with these traces of humanity, or inversely, pleasure taken in the resistance of the material to human transformation. Our enjoyment in other words seizes the cultural aspects of a thing or the natural aspects of a thing, the ideological values of a thing, or the material feel of a thing; or, more likely, the balanced integration of the two, the *gestalt* of form and function.

The integrated approach to cultural studies that I propose asserts design studies as the basis of cultural studies and also as the basis of general education. Our awareness of design is a measure of our awareness of the way that we live now as well as a mark of our means to make the most of it. Naturally such awareness will have sweeping ramifications for the entirety of our economy and society: it will change the way that we interact with and appreciate almost all of the objects of our world.

Design Studies

All of this in mind, let's ask an institutional question, borrowed from Marshall McLuhan: How can we move forward looking back?

At this point we might focus the question on design education or rather, first, on the question of the relationship between design and education. If design is the primary force in culture today, the ground upon which everything else stands or falls, one would expect our educational institutions and the disciplinary discourses that animate them to reorganize themselves or at least to have started reorganizing themselves around problems related to design. This is not to say that every discipline should be reorganized around a base model of strict utilitarianism – conjuring and classifying knowledge only if that knowledge can serve some human endeavor, some question or problem in design. Such an assertion would tap an active and enduring debate between the pure and applied sciences, both of which clearly benefit from the existence of the other and both of which, for this reason, already loosely satisfy our concerns.

Despite the functionalist paradigm that dogs discussions of design, the impact of design far exceeds the limits of utilitarian concern. The question of design is the question of culture, of human experience and meaning, in all of its breadth and complexity. Design decisions create the sphere of human meaning even when that meaning is related to the absence of human presence, as in the preservation of watersheds or of the wilderness.

The disciplines whose mission it is to investigate culture as a sphere of meaning or value are the disciplines of the Humanities – the hermeneutic disciplines as they are sometimes called since their task is to interpret structures of meaning. If the design disciplines are primary agents in the creation of human experience in contemporary culture, and hence also agents shaping the sphere of meaning or value in contemporary culture, the Humanities fields should be concerned with design.

Increasingly, as we have already observed, this is in fact the case. Almost every department on any given university campus has someone or several people studying some aspect of design – historic, contemporary, local, distant or global. Historians and Anthropologists study Material Culture. Sociologists study Consumption, among other design related topics. Literature departments are expanding to include several types of text-image production, from graphic novels to children's books, as well as other design related texts including cookbooks and digital forms like video games. Philosophers explore the philosophy of technology and of science.

By studying design, educators in the Humanities are able to speak to contemporary culture and to contemporary students in a meaningful way. I am not suggesting that educators pander to contemporary concerns: quite the opposite, I'm suggesting that they hold a critical mirror up to it. It is just as easy for professors to teach fluff courses – there are too many! – on obscure, arcane or irrelevant topics within the specialized corners of any given discipline as it is to teach fluff courses on obscure, arcane or irrelevant areas of contemporary culture.

Rather than seeing design studies on the margins of many disciplines across campus it might be more productive, intellectually and administratively, to see design studies as the tie that binds, the non-unitary, utterly heterogeneous *central* concern of the contemporary university.

Our current educational institutions generally affiliate design education with the arts. Some design fields have their own flagship institutions or programs within institutions: fashion and architecture, for example, generally stand apart. Other fields fall under the aegis of art education, though this is slowly changing. It would undoubtedly be interesting to survey art schools and programs today to find out how many have recently changed their names to foreground design: from Art Department to Department of Art and Design or simply Design, as happened a few years ago at PennDesign, at the University of Pennsylvania.

At one institution where I taught, the Department of Art and Design housed programs in Studio Art, including painting, ceramics, metals, and sculpture; Graphic Design; Interior Design; and Art History. Across campus, in an affiliated technical college, a program in print media trained printers, though it had no direct or indirect contact with the graphic design program. By far the lion share of the students in the Department of Art and Design were majoring in either graphic or interior design, as many as 75% at last count. The curriculum for these designers in training required that they take the same foundations or fundamentals courses that studio art majors were required to take and that they spend a certain number of their "elective" hours studying in the other arts. This curriculum was put in place at the insistence of the other programs within the department. The other programs would have been strapped for students if design students weren't required to take courses from them. The benefits of such requirements are of course subject to debate. This isn't the place for a detailed argument about curriculum, but it is interesting to note this aspect of the parasitic rapport that persists between these fields.

Just a few years ago, Art and Design created a course incorporating elements of graphic design history into a larger history of reproducible images, from the woodcut to Photoshop, intended for students pursuing a minor in art history, but no other design history classes were offered and the students didn't have time to take them anyway. The curriculum in graphic design emphasized creative over critical activity almost completely. During their final years in the program students had only one free elective period to fill as they wished and unsurprisingly few were interested in pursuing something different from the rest of their coursework.

I dwell on these institutional structures because they are relatively typical. But this is not to say that changes aren't taking place. More and more art history programs are hiring design critics and historians. And more and more design programs are requiring courses in design history. These changes are undoubtedly good for design history as a specialized field even if they fail to maximize the interest in design studies that can be found in other fields across campus. My point here is that there are design historians in the history department, among other departments, and that administrative structures must be reformed to permit students access to these teachers as well as to permit these teachers to have access to design students.

A shift is taking place in art and design education and the students are essentially leading the charge, undoubtedly for many reasons. As the Fine Art tradition continues to lose its luster, the secular aura of aesthetic genius is shifting to design. Students experience design all around them every day, they swim in it. In such a context, it is natural that they might seek to become designers rather than Fine Artists – Romantic creators whose works are sequestered in marble mausoleums in far off cultural "capitals." Today's students are also computer savvy in an entirely new way. This is important in the design fields, which now rely so heavily on technology. For students who love to work with computers, design offers a way of working with computers that is also a way of making things in the world, a means of creating and interacting. And of course, designers also make money.

The image of the starving artist is as unappealing to many of today's students as it is to their parents.

It is one thing to say that enrollments are up in design and quite another to suggest that these students are being adequately prepared for their role in shaping our culture. Sending more students through the same antiquated system is no way to move forward. Cultural conditions have changed, changing enrollments, and hopefully curriculums will change with them.

I'd like to propose something still more sweeping: a new approach to cultural economy, for designers and for everyone else, an approach focused on material forms and the experiences – physical, intellectual and otherwise – that they help create. Such an approach would highlight the way that design decisions create culture and thereby it would also highlight the interaction between the human and natural worlds.

Suppose we stop and actually take a close look at our lived environment to determine the precise nature of the forces that shape that environment and act upon us within it? Such an inquiry is fraught with complications, some needless, some not. What do we mean by lived environment, by *forces* and by the notion that those forces may at once shape the environment and shape us, holding out that these processes may not be commensurate or even related? Such an inquiry proposes a clear and close look at the world around us unveiled by anticipation or interest, it proposes that we attempt to see the world for what it is, without mistaking our place or role within it through either under- or over-estimation.

The proposition here is that of an interdisciplinary approach to culture organized around the material forms of the way we live, which is to say questions of design. Such an approach would incorporate the lessons of the radical critique of Western civilization, a phrase understood in its fullest sense as the diverse culture of globalization, since the West has spread its ideology and cultural forms and technologies around the world through globalization. Unfortunately this critique has deteriorated, to a large extent, into the politically correct proclamations and pursuits of what has been called the School of Resentment, the pursuit of diversity for its own sake. The radical critique of Western civilization began with the critique of representation – in idealist forms of philosophy, religion, and science (Nietzsche), economics (Marx), and psychology (Freud) – but, rather than abandoning faith in representation, many of our institutions have intensified an endeavor to merely diversify the cultural encyclopedia rather than to abolish it.

We have entered into a new phase of cultural history defined by a new cultural economy, a cultural economy given shape by design. We need to develop new fields of cultural study based on the material facts of the way that we actually live, new approaches to materialogy, topology, grammatology: the things, places, and rhetoric of design. Since the design fields are themselves complex rather than unitary, this is not an appeal to apply any one analytic model to cultural production as a whole, nor even a claim that cultural production can be understood as a whole. The design fields are themselves diverse, internally and externally, and they collaborate and collide in culture in a manner that cannot be subsumed under the sign of hegemony. Contributors to a common cause – creating the context of everyday life – the design fields cannot assert themselves, independently or as a whole, as isolated or efficient causes or effects of culture. For this reason they are often hard to see. But see them we must, if we are to understand the way that we live now and to improve our chances of living well in the future.